The Gospel

THE KINGDOM APPREHENDED

The Gospel

THE KINGDOM APPREHENDED

RICHARD BARTHOLOMEE

A Division of WINEPRESS PUBLISHING

Pleasant Word (a division of WinePress Publishing, PO Box 428, Enumclaw, WA 98022) functions only as book publisher. As such, the ultimate design, content, editorial accuracy, and views expressed or implied in this work are those of the author.

Unless otherwise noted, all Scriptures are taken from the *New American Standard Bible*, © 1960, 1963, 1968, 1971, 1972, 1973, 1975, 1977 by The Lockman Foundation. Used by permission.

ISBN 13: 978-1-4141-1117-9
ISBN 10: 1-4141-1117-7
Library of Congress Catalog Card Number: 2007907691

THE
GOSPEL

To the church, the body of Christ, the redeemed,
and to those who need to be

Richard G. Bartholomee

"And I saw another angel flying in midheaven, having an eternal
Gospel to preach to those who live on the earth, and to every nation
and tribe and tongue and people."

—Revelation 14:6

Contents

Preface

For some time now, and more intensely so for the past year, the Lord has laid a burden on my heart to write on the subject of the Kingdom of God. Not being an author of any renown, in the past I have written some articles, mostly religious and unpublished except for a few in Christian magazines. However, this intense prompting to write on such an important subject simply would not abate, and so an earnest study of the Scriptures ensued. I found myself enthralled with the reality of just how much the Bible has to say concerning the Kingdom of God.

While wrestling with the thought of why I of all people should start writing such a work at the age of 76—now finishing it at age 77—I was reminded of something E. Stanley Jones was told when he was 86. William S. McBirnie told him that he should write a book on the subject of the Kingdom of God. And when Jones asked, "Why me?" he was told, "Because you are in the Kingdom of God, and the Kingdom of God is in you." Whereupon Jones promised to study the subject for a year, and if after that time he felt led to write on the subject, he would. The result was his book *The Unshakable Kingdom and the Unchanging Person.*

If the passion which engulfed my late brother in the Lord after his year of study could propel him at the age of 87 to produce such a fine masterpiece, perhaps there might be some hope that I too may have caught some of that passion. I can only pray that if by some chance you get to read this treatise, it will cause a deep desire in your heart to know more about the magnificent Kingdom of God and its King.

At first glance this may well seem to be a very short treatise on such a vast subject. However, if you will follow my suggestions, I am certain that you will find this to be a richly rewarding adventure. In this regard, may I urge you to read not only what I have attempted to put down in print, but ever so more importantly, *every Bible reference given as you go along.* I believe it will make all the difference.

If I have in any way been able to convey to you what He has conveyed to me, then my task will have proven to be a success. If for any reason I have missed the mark somewhere in my musings, please let me know so that I may grow in a better understanding of the King and His Kingdom.

Richard G. Bartholomee
January 4, 2007

Acknowledgments

First and foremost, my deepest gratitude to the King and His Holy Spirit for planting in my heart the deep desire to learn more about the Gospel of the Kingdom of God, answering my many prayers, showing me the way step by step, and allowing me the opportunity to put those discoveries and thoughts in writing.

Next, my heartfelt thanks to one of my co-laborers in the Kingdom, Harold Linville, for all his assistance in helping me search the Scriptures and providing me with invaluable information, insight, and encouragement every step of the way in this remarkable adventure.

And finally, my love and appreciation to my long-suffering, beautiful wife, Helen, who has made it possible for me to spend so much time in these latter years of my life pursuing my vision and dream. Thank you. What a blessing you are to me. You are the ideal help mate and one in whom the love of the Lord is apparent to all who know you. And what a special blessing from the Lord to me to be able to complete this labor of love on our 44th wedding anniversary. I love you.

The Gospel
Part One

The Gospel. Good news, yes, but of what? For the most part, have we not missed the mark in understanding the reality of what took place some 2,000 years ago? Time now to discover, perhaps for the first time, the truth about the Gospel.

The Gospel begins with the announcement by the angel, Gabriel, to a young virgin maiden of the Lord, Mary or Miriam. He greeted her with words strange to her ears by saying that she was a woman highly favored or blessed by the Lord—that she would conceive by the power of the Holy Spirit and bear a son to be named Jesus, who would be called the Son of God. This Jesus, Gabriel said, "will be great and will be called the Son of the Most High; and the Lord God will give Him the throne of His father, David; and He will reign over the house of Jacob forever, and His Kingdom will have no end."[1]

Months later, this profound announcement was followed by another angelic visitation, this time to shepherds in the field watching over their flocks. The glory of the Lord suddenly appeared all around them as the angel proclaimed, "I bring you good news of great joy which will be for all people; for today in the City of David there has been born for you a Savior, who is Christ the Lord." Once announced, the whole sky was filled with a multitude of the heavenly host, all praising the one true and living God and loudly proclaiming, "Glory to God in the highest, and upon earth peace among men of good will."[2] What an awesome moment in time. From this moment on the world would never be the same, because heaven had come to earth in the Person of the only begotten Son of God!

Who is this Savior for all the people? He is none other than the long-awaited Messiah, the one who would crush the head of the serpent, Satan, as promised by Almighty God to Adam and Eve in the Garden of Eden.[3] This is the very one spoken of by the very same Gabriel to the prophet Daniel as the Messiah;[4] the one proclaimed to be the Lamb of God who takes away the sin of the world by John the baptizer;[5] the Messiah declared to have been found by Andrew, the brother of Simon Peter;[6] the one who was anticipated by the Samaritan woman at the well to come someday;[7] He who was referred to by King David as the King of glory;[8] the one spoken of as the King of the Jews by the magi from the east;[9] and finally and definitively declared to be "the blessed and only Sovereign, the King of kings and Lord of Lords."[10] King Jesus! This is not merely good news. It is the best, most important, glorious news ever to be proclaimed!

If one is to be a king, then there must of necessity be a kingdom over which he is to rule and reign. And, if Jesus is the King of all kings, of what must His Kingdom consist? The King and His Kingdom is the subject of this treatise. This then is *the Gospel*. This is the good news which Paul declared in his day to have been "proclaimed in all creation under heaven."[11] And this is the good news which King Jesus has commanded that His followers preach to all creation even now.[12] What better way to understand the full impact and meaning of the Gospel than to start at the point in time when Jesus is about to make His appearance, no longer as a baby in an animal feeding trough, or as a young boy astounding the religious teachers of His day in Jerusalem, but now as the Son of man.

When John the baptizer first came on the scene preparing the way for the coming of the Lord, he actually gave us the first glimpse of what the Gospel was all about. He began preaching in the wilderness, and multitudes flocked to him from all over Judea to hear what he had to say. His message was a simple one. He said, "Repent, for the Kingdom of Heaven is at hand."[13] To a nation now being dominated by pagans in and from Rome, this proclamation that the Kingdom of God was about to make its appearance must have been the greatest possible news to the ears of those downtrodden Israelites.

After John had declared Jesus to be the Lamb of God who takes away the sin of the world[14], Jesus, following His baptism and temptation in the wilderness, began His ministry. What was His original message? It was identical to that of His forerunner, John, for He too proclaimed, "Repent, for the Kingdom of Heaven is at hand."[15] That which the prophets of old had desired to see centuries before was soon to be made manifest.[16] The Kingdom of God was about to invade the earth.[17] Exciting news indeed!

In the days Jesus walked the earth ministering to His disciples and to the multitudes, this then was the Gospel. "And(Jesus) was going about in all Galilee(all of the cities and villages), teaching in their synagogues, and proclaiming the Gospel of the Kingdom, and healing every kind of disease and every kind of sickness among the people."[18] From the outset, and all through those three and a half years of His ministry, the emphasis of His teaching was centered on the fact that the Kingdom of God had come, first of all in the form of the King Himself, but soon to be populated with multitudes of people throughout the entire world. In His discourse on the mountain, for instance, Jesus referred to this invasion of heaven upon the earth. He said, "Blessed(are) you(who are) poor, for yours *is* the Kingdom of Heaven."[19] And again, "Blessed are those who have been persecuted for the sake of righteousness, for theirs *is* the Kingdom of Heaven."[20] Notice that these promises are in the present tense, as well as giving future assurance. As the beloved hymn of

Fanny J. Crosby proclaims, "Blessed assurance, Jesus is mine! O what a foretaste of glory divine!" Present and future is this Kingdom.

Of course, the Gospel of the Kingdom of God is not confined to the one statement, "Repent, for the Kingdom of God is at hand." For instance, Jesus often spoke in parables when addressing the crowds—especially when those crowds included the religious leaders of the day. Many of those parables described the Kingdom of God in difficult terms for those who were dull of heart to understand. Often His parables were even difficult for His eager students to understand. However, He delighted to share with His disciples the mysteries of the Kingdom of Heaven.[21]

We will examine some of the parables in greater detail later. But for now it is sufficient to point out that Jesus presented the Kingdom of God as the singular most important, costly, and precious possession one could ever desire. He spoke of it as a hidden treasure[22] and as a pearl of great price.[23] When some of those parables were difficult, even for His chosen disciples, Jesus would explain them in great detail, assuring them that it was the good pleasure of their heavenly Father to give them the Kingdom of God.[24] The privilege of sharing with Him the Kingdom of Heaven was being given to them!

They were to be the recipients of this great gift from the throne of God—but not just for them alone. Abba Father desired for them to share the Gospel of His Kingdom on earth with others. Shortly after the twelve apostles were chosen by Jesus, He sent them out in pairs to the lost sheep of Israel, giving them authority to freely cast out demons, heal all manner of sicknesses and diseases—including the dreaded disease of leprosy—and causing the lame to walk, the blind to see, and to even raise the dead—all the miracles in fact which He Himself was performing. His instructions to them were clear. They were not only given the authority to heal the bodies of these Israelites, but they were to proclaim to the peoples of the land that they were to repent, for "the Kingdom of Heaven has come near."[25]

A short time later Jesus sent out seventy others of His disciples, again two by two, to every city and location where He Himself intended to visit. His instructions to them were the same. They were to heal the sick and to proclaim the Gospel to the people in these words, "the Kingdom of God has come near to you."[26] Jesus had given these disciples all power and authority over Satan and his demons. They returned filled with joy and awe because of the power they were able to exercise—especially over the servants of Satan. Jesus assured them that their names had been recorded in Heaven. He Himself rejoiced at their reports of having seen Satan fall from Heaven, praising Abba Father for hiding the things concerning the Gospel of the Kingdom of God from those who in their own minds were the wise and among the intelligentsia of society, and, instead, revealing these mysteries of His Kingdom to those who would receive them as little children.[27]

That authority given by Jesus to the twelve and to the seventy to proclaim the Gospel of the Kingdom of God to the children of Israel has now been given to all believers everywhere. After His resurrection and before joining His Father in heaven to sit at His right hand, Jesus instructed His disciples to go into all the world and preach this Gospel of the Kingdom of God to all creation, baptizing them in the name of the Father, Son, and Holy Spirit, and teaching them to observe all that He had taught and commanded them. He promised that He would be with them and that signs or attesting miracles would accompany those who believed in His name, and that every believer would be able to cast out demons, speak with new tongues, heal the sick, and not be harmed by the forces of Satan.[28] Just before Jesus was lifted up into Heaven, and to be certain that His disciples understood the full impact of His Gospel and how far and wide it was to be proclaimed, He told them that they were to be His witnesses, not only in Jerusalem, Judea, and Samaria, but even to the remotest parts of the earth—to all peoples everywhere.[29] In fact, Jesus had previously told His disciples that before the end of the world would come, "this Gospel of the Kingdom shall be proclaimed in the whole world."[30]

Turning now to the King's specific teachings concerning His Kingdom, we begin with some of the parables. Jesus spoke in simple and practical, yet profound, ways concerning His Kingdom. Take for instance the parable of the sower of the seed.[31] Some of the seed fell beside the road, others on rocky places, some among the thorns, but others fell on good soil. Unless the seed fell on good soil, the seed would not produce what it was designed to produce. Instead, it would be eaten by birds, or scorched in the sun because of a lack of soil, or choked out by thorns. Jesus explained to His disciples that the seed represented the Gospel of the Kingdom of God, and the various places where it fell represented the hearts of the people addressed. To those who will not keep pressing in until they have understood, the enemy will remove the truth from their hearts. To those whose hearts have become filled with stones, they will receive the words of truth at first, even with great joy, but they have no heart left to persevere over the problems which they face, and they lose heart. Others may hear the Gospel, but they are more concerned with the things of the world, such as wealth and power, not realizing that they are passing up the most valuable possession in the world, the Kingdom of God. But to those who will cling to the King and His word and His way, they will go on and multiply, showing to others the way to His Kingdom.

Using the same metaphor of seed, Jesus presents another parable concerning the Kingdom of Heaven. Good wheat seed(being the sons of the Kingdom of God) are sown by Jesus, the Son of man, into His field(which is the world). But along comes the great counterfeiter, the devil, and he causes to be planted seeds which resemble wheat, but which in reality are weeds. These seeds are the sons of Satan. Only when the plants are mature can one more easily distinguish for themselves the difference between the good and the evil. The men of God inquire of the Master whether they should set out to destroy the unrighteous ones in their midst. But the Master is concerned that man, no matter how righteous and well-intended, in the process of removing the evil ones, might harm or destroy some of the faithful. He assures them that the sons of Satan will be dealt with at the end of the age by angels sent from Heaven. At the command of Jesus His angels will gather the evil ones out of the Kingdom of God, leaving the sons and daughters of righteousness to rule and reign with Him in His Kingdom.[32]

This parable reveals, again, an important truth. The Kingdom of God is both present and future. When the Gospel is proclaimed in all its fullness and received in the hearts of those who hear, the windows of Heaven are opened and the Kingdom of God is born in their midst. After John the baptizer had been imprisoned, Jesus proclaimed the Gospel of God in Galilee, saying, "The time is fulfilled, and the Kingdom of God has come near; repent and believe in the Gospel."[33] During this time, while being accompanied by His disciples, Jesus addressed the crowd, saying, "Truly I say to you, there are some of those who are standing here who will not taste death until they see the Kingdom of God after it has come with power."[34]

Surely Jesus had reference to the time when His personal ministry on earth had come to an end culminating in His death on the cross, burial in a borrowed tomb, and His glorious resurrection, and when His closest disciples were gathered together in Jerusalem on the day of Pentecost. The door of Heaven suddenly opened wide invading the house where they sat in fear of the religious authorities. With a loud noise like thunder and tongues of fire coming upon them, they were filled with the Holy Spirit. The Kingdom of God had come with power![35]

Previously, and perhaps as a foretaste of things to come, Jesus had taken three of His disciples—Peter, James and John—to a high mountain where He was gloriously transfigured before them. He was arrayed in radiant white garments, and appearing with Him were the prophet Elijah and the leader of the Israelites, Moses. What a sight to behold! Peter was so overwhelmed that he wanted at once to build three tabernacles, one for each of them. But Abba Father spoke from Heaven proclaiming that Jesus was His beloved Son, and He was the one to whom they should listen.[36] This Jesus was to be received as the King of Abba's Kingdom.

When speaking to the crowds, Jesus spoke in parables—revealing to some and, at the same time, hiding from others, things that were hidden from man since the very foundation of the world.[37] Time and again He tried to convey the mystery of this glorious, earth-changing Gospel, the Gospel of the Kingdom of God. He spoke of it as a treasure of such great magnitude that the one who found it—hidden from sight in a field—was so filled with joy he sold everything he owned so as to be able to purchase the field in which this treasure was hidden.[38] No possession on earth is its equal. Even to one who had spent his whole life dealing in the very finest of pearls to be found anywhere, when he found this one pearl of such great price, incapable of being evaluated in worldly terms, took his entire life's collection of costly gems and sold them all in order to be able to possess this priceless treasure.[39] In the first case, the man seemed to find this treasure almost by accident. To the pearl merchant, he was searching for that one pearl that would outshine all others. Jesus makes it clear that nothing on this earth is worth pursuing more than entering into the Kingdom of God. And the good news (or Gospel) is that it is available to all who will hear and believe.

One of the great paradoxes in the uncovering of the mysteries of this greatest discovery of all time as portrayed in the above parables is that while the Kingdom of God is a free gift from Him, it will cost you everything you have and are. Should this cause anyone to be anxious, Jesus teaches us not to be anxious for anything, including what we shall eat or drink or what clothing we wear. Rather, He tells us that we are to continually seek first His Kingdom and His righteousness, and our heavenly Father, who knows our every need, will see to all those physical needs.[40] Is the Kingdom of God costly? Yes. And at the same time it is the free gift of God. As Jesus said to His disciples, "Do not be afraid, little flock, for your Father has chosen gladly to give you the Kingdom."[41]

Other parables of Jesus present the Kingdom of Heaven in various forms. He likened it to a tiny mustard seed, the smallest of all seeds, but when planted in good soil it becomes a strong, tall, and stately tree, providing shelter and safety to the birds of the air.[42] The Gospel of the Kingdom of God may seem to many a small and insignificant matter, but in reality it is the one thing that can bring peace and safety to all who enter in.

Jesus likewise likened the Kingdom of God to leaven or yeast, which in and of itself is very small. However, when it is mixed with dough, it grows a hundredfold and leavens the whole loaf.[43] Leaven does not have to be evil, such as the leaven of the scribes and Pharisees. It can also be good and righteous—its truth producing in the hearts of mankind the Kingdom of God.

There is another parable of Jesus concerning the Kingdom of God. This one may be a bit more difficult at first to understand, but the understanding of it will bring great blessings. He said that the Kingdom of Heaven was like a dragnet cast into the sea gathering all kinds of fish. When the net was full, the good fish were preserved, but the bad fish were cast away. Jesus went on to explain in the parable that at the consummation of this age His angels would be sent to remove the wicked from the righteous, throwing the wicked, who will be weeping and gnashing their teeth, into the very fires of hell.[44] This sounds very similar to His parable concerning the good seed and the tares, the angels being the ones to separate the good from the evil. Jesus often presented truth in different forms in order that it would be understood by all those who were truly called of God. That is one of the basic reasons for all the parables explaining the Kingdom of God.

This parable seems to be the last in this particular series concerning the Kingdom of God, and after presenting it, He asked His disciples if they understood all of these parables, and they immediately replied in the affirmative.[45] The Lord desires for us to understand all things concerning His Kingdom. In this parable Jesus makes it clear that there are those who give the appearance of being sons and daughters of the Kingdom who will in the final analysis be cast away. This is a difficult conclusion to have to draw, but one which must be faced honestly. An example of this is found in the conclusion of the account where Jesus deals with a certain officer in the Roman army.

When entering Capernaum on one occasion, Jesus was approached by a Roman centurion on behalf of his son who had been thrown down on the ground, presumably by a demonic force, and was in torment. Jesus offered to go to the home of the centurion and heal his son, but the centurion would not hear of it. Why? First of all, it was the custom and tradition of the religious leaders of the day that a Jew should not ever enter the house of a Gentile because for it would make the Jew unclean, and Jesus would therefore be violating this custom in the eyes of those religious leaders. Rest assured, that would not have deterred Jesus from going to his home. However, the centurion, being a humble man, believed himself to be unworthy of such a visit from a person of such higher rank than he. He, being a man under the authority of Caesar, recognized that Jesus was under the authority of someone far greater than Caesar, Almighty God Himself. And yet the condition and fate of his son compelled him to present his plea for healing to Jesus. Notice, however, how he went about it. He asked Jesus to just speak the word, knowing that His mere word would be sufficient for his son to be delivered from his malady.

Jesus was amazed at the faith of the Roman, and said, "Truly I say to you, I have not found such great faith with anyone in Israel." He went on to state, and herein lies a sober truth about the Kingdom of God, that there would be many Gentiles who would dine at the great supper with Abraham, Isaac, and Jacob in the Kingdom of Heaven, but that many of the sons of the Kingdom, Israelites by birth, would be cast out of His Kingdom into the very pit of hell.[46] What is it in the final analysis that will determine who stays in the Kingdom of God and who will be removed? In a word, righteousness. Did not Jesus say that we were not only to seek first His Kingdom, but also His righteousness? And what is righteousness? We are told that Abraham believed God, and God counted that faith in Him as righteousness. Abraham did not just believe in God; he believed God. So did this Roman centurion.

Back to our parable of the dragnet. There are many of His own who did not recognize Jesus as their Messiah—especially those of the religious leaders of the day. They either ignored or were ignorant of the promise of God to send a Redeemer as revealed by Moses and the prophets. But, as indicated by Jesus, there would be those even of the scribes who would recognize from the Scriptures that He indeed was the one who was prophesied, and that they would enter into and become disciples of the Kingdom of Heaven, drawing from the prophesies and teachings of old, and combining them with the word now being taught by Jesus. In other words, they believed God—Abba Father would reckon their faith in the Messiah as righteousness, just as He had with Abraham and the Roman centurion.

Jesus confirmed this principle when dealing with Thomas, who demanded to see and touch the nail prints in His hands and the wound in His side before he would believe that Jesus really was Lord and God, and that He had been raised from the dead. Appearing to Thomas, as He had already previously appeared to the others, actually seeing and touching His wounds made a believer of Thomas. However, Jesus said to him, "Because you have seen Me, have you believed? Blessed are they who did not see, and yet believed."[47] This then is true righteousness.

In my judgment, it simply is not possible for us to devote too much time in studying the subject of the Gospel of the Kingdom of God. After all, it is the one singular most important subject in the Bible, from Genesis through Revelation. Especially this is true of the New Testament, from the Gospel accounts to the revelation of Jesus as presented to the apostle John. Think about it. The Gospels open with the proclamation that the Kingdom of God has arrived, first in the birth of its King;[48] then in the preaching of John the baptizer;[49] followed by the preaching of the King Himself.[50] From the beginning of His ministry here on earth to the very end before He ascended into Heaven to sit at the right hand of His Father, Jesus continually proclaimed the Gospel of the Kingdom of God, in the parables as we have seen, and in clear, unmistakable terms as we shall consider shortly. But, for the moment, consider what the Master said before departing for Heaven.

As we have seen, at the close of the Gospel account, Jesus gave specific instructions to those called to be the sons of the Kingdom to preach this Gospel of His Kingdom to all creation,[51] causing disciples from all nations to become fellow heirs of His Kingdom.[52] Throughout the pages of the four Gospel accounts the singular common theme of Jesus' teaching is the Gospel of the Kingdom of God. He spoke of it no less than one hundred recorded times Himself. Nor did the message of the Kingdom end with the Gospel accounts. After His resurrection, and in His transformed body, Jesus spent some forty days with His disciples. And what exactly was He speaking to them about during those forty days? He spoke "of things concerning the Kingdom of God."[53]

Even so, His disciples still did not get it, because just before He left them, they were asking Him if this was the time when He would restore the kingdom to Israel.[54] Their thinking was much too small. They were only concerned with the kingdom of one country—their beloved Israel. Their vision would have to be greatly enlarged to understand the true meaning of the Kingdom of God. May I suggest that our concern and vision may also be far too small when it comes to things pertaining to the Kingdom of God. Is not our concern far too often whether our church will be recognized as the one true church of the Lord, and other churches and denominations will be exposed for the error of their ways? Consider this fact. Jesus only used the term "church" on two occasions throughout the entire four Gospel accounts. The first is found when Peter, receiving revelation from the Father in Heaven, declared that Jesus was the Messiah, the Son of the living God. Upon his confession of this great truth, Jesus told Peter and the rest that on the basis of this truth, "I will build My church, and the gates of Hades will not overpower it."[55] But notice in His very next breath, Jesus told Peter, "I will give you the keys of the Kingdom of Heaven, and whatever you bind on earth shall have been bound in Heaven, and whatever you loose on earth shall have been loosed in Heaven."[56] Even here, however, and in this very context, Jesus placed the emphasis, not on the church but rather on the Kingdom of God.

The only other time that Jesus used the term "church" was when He was teaching His disciples about discipline within His body. He instructed them(and us) that if a member of His body sins, for us to go to him alone and show him his fault. If he will not listen to you, take one or two witnesses with you and try to win your brother again. If he will not listen to you or the witnesses, then, and only then, are you to tell it to the church.[57] These steps are taken in order to, if at all possible, bring the brother(or sister) to repentance and to be restored to proper relationship with the Lord and His body.

Again, these are the only two occasions when Jesus used the term "church." Contrast this with the fact, if you will, that He used the terms "Kingdom of Heaven" or "Kingdom of God"(these terms are synonymous, as a comparison of Matthew 13:31-33 and Luke 13:18-21, for example, will show) more than one hundred times in His teachings. Have we perhaps spent far too much time talking about the church and not nearly enough time talking about what He talked at length about—the Gospel of the Kingdom of God?

Before ascending to heaven to sit at His Father's right hand, Jesus instructed His followers to wait in Jerusalem until they had received the necessary power from Heaven so as to be able to proclaim the full Gospel of the Kingdom of God. Once they had this power from on high, they were to be witnesses of the King and His Kingdom, not only in Jerusalem, Judea and Samaria, but to the remotest parts of the earth. [58] They would then be able to comprehend the full significance of the Kingdom of God on earth.

Jesus had stated clearly that the Gospel of the Kingdom of God was to be proclaimed in the entire world.[59] We see this being at least partially fulfilled throughout the entire pages of the Book of the Acts of the Apostles. In fact, see how that book begins and closes. It begins, as we have said, with Jesus, in His resurrected body, spending forty days with His disciples, discussing at length things concerning the Kingdom of God.[60] The book of Acts closes with the apostle Paul in Rome, in what we would probably describe as house arrest in his own quarters, and for the past two years while awaiting trial before Caesar, we are told, that he welcomed all who came to visit him, "proclaiming the Kingdom of God and teaching concerning Jesus," the King of that Kingdom.[61] The King and His kingdom—*the Gospel!*

End of Part One. Respectfully submitted for your study, prayer and consideration. May 31, 2006.

The Gospel
Part Two

B efore proceeding further in our study of the Gospel of the Kingdom of God, there perhaps needs to be some clarification of the statements made in Part One of this treatise concerning the term "church." In no way was it the intention of this author to denigrate the church of the Lord. On the contrary, we need to take very seriously the true concept of the church as espoused by the Lord Himself. Jesus stated that on the basis of the fact that He was the Messiah, the Son of the living God, He would build His church, and that the gates of hell would not be able to overpower it.[1] The building of the Lord's church is an extremely important doctrine to understand.

First and foremost, notice that the Lord made it clear as to who would build His church. Man would not build it. Jesus Himself would build it. As we observe the existence today of denominations—literally numbering in the thousands—is it possible that man has attempted to usurp the authority which the Lord has reserved unto Himself? Where do we find, then, the authority for the existence of these man-made denominations? The truth of the matter lies in the fact that there is only one church authorized by Abba Father and Heaven itself, and that is the church which Jesus Himself promised to build, His body here on earth.

The Lord's plan was to have one church for one community—regardless of the number of homes in that community in which the members might meet. How can we know? Consider the Lord's own letters to seven specific churches in seven specific cities recorded for us in Chapters 2 and 3 of the Book of Revelation. It is this one church for one community which the apostle Paul addresses in his letters.[2]

Jesus declared that all authority had been given to Him, both in Heaven and on the earth.[3] It is essential that His church, His body on the earth, be one. How can we know this to be true? By the very plea of Jesus to the Father on behalf of His disciples when He prayed, "I do not ask on behalf of these alone, but for those also who believe in Me through their word; that they may all be one; even as You, Father, are in Me and I in You, that they also may be in Us, so that the world may continually believe that You sent Me. The glory which You have given Me I have given to them, that they may be one, just as We are one; I in them and You in Me, that they may be perfected into one, so that the world may continually know that You sent Me, and loved them, even as You have loved Me."[4]

And how can we possibly be one in Him as He is in the Father if we continue to be so divided and separate from one another in our institutions and organizations formed by man? Paul, the apostle, describes the Lord's church as a single organism or body, formed by Jesus Himself and His Father in Heaven.[5] Can we not be just members of His body, His church, and thus do our part in bringing about the fulfillment of our Lord's prayer? So much depends on our ability to do His will in this regard, and allow Him, and Him alone, to build His church.

What does this have to do with the Gospel of the Kingdom of God on the earth? Much in every way. Do you recall what Jesus said to the chief priests and the elders of the people of Israel when His authority and teaching was challenged by them?[6] He presented to them yet two more of His parables. The first of these was the parable of a man's two children whom the father instructed to work in his vineyard. The first refused, but later thought better of his decision and went to work in the vineyard. The second child promised to work in the vineyard but failed to do so. Jesus wanted to know which child had done the father's will. The religious leaders rightfully said that it was the first child.

Prior to telling this parable, Jesus, in response to their questioning Him by what or whose authority He did the things He did and taught in the manner in which He taught, asked them about the baptism of John; was it by the authority of men or God? They reasoned among themselves that if they said it was by God's authority, they would have to give some explanation as to why had they not been obedient to it themselves? But if they insisted that it was not of God, but man, then they would be in trouble with the crowd, who regarded John as a prophet of God. The answer was an easy one. The baptism of John was from the throne room of Heaven to prepare the way for the coming of the Messiah and His Kingdom.

Jesus went on to tell them that sinners believed John, and therefore they were entering the Kingdom of God, but that they, refusing to repent like the first child in the parable, would not enter into His Kingdom. Jesus knew how this would be received by these religious leaders, so He told them another parable of a man who owned a vineyard and leased it out to vine-growers. When the harvest came, he sent his slaves to collect his share of the harvest. Each time he tried to collect his just dues, the vine-growers not only refused to pay, but beat or killed the slaves who came to collect. Finally, the owner sent his son, fully expecting the vine-growers to respect him, but instead, they killed the son and attempted to seize the son's inheritance by force. Jesus then asked these religious leaders what would happen when the owner himself came. Again, their answer was true to the mark. They said the owner would give the vine-growers his form of justice, and lease his vineyard to vine-growers who would do right by him.

Without their knowing, Jesus was prophesying that they, the religious leaders themselves, would soon be calling for His death and refusing to receive the Son which the Father above was sending them. They were rejecting the Anointed One of God, their Messiah. After making it clear to them that they were rejecting the chief corner stone of the Kingdom, their reaction was exactly how Jesus had described in the parable; they sought to seize Him and destroy Him.

Careful consideration of this teaching of Jesus is of utmost importance in understanding a vital truth concerning both the church and the Kingdom of God. Give special notice to what Jesus said at the conclusion of these two parables. He said, "Therefore I say to you, the Kingdom of God will be taken away from you and given to a nation producing the fruit of it."[7] Jesus is clearly stating that the Kingdom of God and access to it would be taken from these religious leaders of the nation of Israel and given to another nation who would be worthy of it.

Why was the nation of Israel under its present leadership no longer worthy to bring the gospel of the Kingdom of God to the world? To answer this question one must at least briefly review and analyze how Almighty God created a nation from the loins of one man, Abraham, His purpose in creating that nation, and the impact God desired for that nation to have on the entire world.

After promising Abraham that his descendants would number as the stars of the heavens and the sands of the seashore,[8] God promised that his descendants would be given all the land from the Nile River in Egypt to the Euphrates River—land previously occupied by numerous tribes and nations.[9] That promise was passed on to Abraham's son of promise, Isaac, and then on to his son, Jacob, and through Jacob(whose name was changed by Abba Father to Israel)[10] on down to his twelve sons—giving birth to what would be known as the nation of Israel. Hear the words of God as He renewed His promise to Abraham and Isaac, now directed to Jacob(Israel) and his sons:

> I am God Almighty(El Shaddai); be fruitful and multiply; a nation and a company of nations shall come into being from you, and kings shall come forth from your loins. The land which I gave to Abraham and Isaac I will give to you, and I will give the land to your seed after you.[11]

Before this promise of God would be fulfilled in Israel and his sons, God had already revealed to Abraham that these descendants of his would be held captive as slaves in the land of Egypt for four hundred years.[12]

What was God's purpose in creating the nation of Israel? He desired to have a nation or people who would receive Him as their King, live by His Kingdom principles as outlined in the commandments handed down personally by Him through His servant Moses, as he in turn received them on Mount Sinai.[13] God was quite specific as to His purpose in creating the nation of Israel. He had already shown them how He had by His own hand delivered them from slavery, destroying their enemies and seeing that they were reimbursed for the years of their forced labor—just as He had promised Abraham He would do.[14]

Now He made them another promise, "…if you will indeed obey My voice and keep My covenant, then you shall be My own possession(or special treasure) among all the peoples, for all the earth is Mine, and you shall be to Me a kingdom of priests and a holy nation."[15] And what was the response of the people? "All that the Lord has spoken we will do!"[16] But did they? No. Time and again they turned away from their King and played the harlot with other gods and peoples, doing what seemed right in their own eyes but not in the eyes of their King. The pages of the book of the Judges attest to this fact. Time after time God would forgive them and restore to them their fortunes as His people cried out to Him for mercy.

But finally the time came when the sons of Israel rejected Almighty God as their King and demanded for themselves an earthly king just like the other nations around them.[17] Instead of being a kingdom of priests and a holy nation, an example to all nations so that those nations could know the blessings of a real King and His Kingdom, they desired instead to be followers of evil rather than leaders of righteousness.

And so, the sons of Israel began to be ruled by earthly kings, some of whom did, or attempted to do, what was right in the sight of their true King, such as David, a man after God's own heart, with whom God made

19

covenant that his kingdom and throne would be established forever.[18] Solomon pleased the Lord in asking Him for an understanding and discerning heart so as to be able to judge the nation of Israel.[19] Hezekiah followed in the footsteps of David, trusting in the Lord, clinging to Him, and keeping His commandments.[20] And Josiah proved to be steadfast in following in the way of David and the Lord.[21] When these kings followed the true King, the Lord blessed them and prospered the land. But there were other kings who rebelled against God and His Kingdom principles, such as the very first king appointed to Israel, Saul.[22] And there followed a host of other kings who rebelled against the true King of Israel doing abominable things in His sight, such as Jeroboam[23], Omri[24], and Ahab[25].

In spite of all the rebellion, the Lord God continued to love His people Israel. He would discipline them when they rebelled, but when they repented of their evil ways, He was quick to forgive them and to prosper them once again. When the promised Messiah came on the scene, Israel was no longer ruled by kings chosen by them or by God. Instead, they were trodden under by the stern hand and heel of Caesar of Rome and the puppets ordained by him. Israel's true King was giving them one more chance. He was sending the Anointed One, His only begotten Son, their long-awaited Messiah promised to them by none other than the one they claimed to follow, Moses. Their beloved Moses had told them, "The Lord your God will raise up for you a prophet like me from among you, from your brothers, you shall listen to him."[26]

And who would that prophet be? None other than Jesus, who is not only the promised Prophet[27], but also Priest[28] and King[29]. (Please take the time to review these noted passages of Scripture making reference to Jesus as Prophet, Priest, and King. You will be blessed.) Here indeed was their King. Moses had instructed them to be sure to listen to Him. But did they, those who were the leaders and teachers of Israel? No. Rather, it was as Jesus said to them, "But woe to you, scribes and Pharisees, hypocrites, because you shut off the Kingdom of Heaven in front of people; for you do not enter in yourselves, nor do you allow those who are entering to go in."[30] And so, as we have seen,[31] Jesus tells them that the Kingdom of God would be taken from them and given to another nation who would be worthy of it and blessed by it.

Another nation? What other nation? Would there be a nation worthy of possessing the Kingdom of God on the earth? Yes! The very stone which the builders rejected, Jesus, would be the chief corner stone of that Kingdom. And which nation would receive Him as King and in so doing be given His Kingdom?

Consider carefully the words of Peter, the apostle—the one to whom Jesus gave the keys to His Kingdom—as he writes to the church, the body of Christ, an organism created by Jesus and composed of the Jew first and also of the Gentile, "But you are a chosen race, a royal priesthood, *a holy nation*, a people for God's own possession, so that you may proclaim the excellencies of Him who has called you out of darkness into His marvelous light; for you once were not a people (nation), but now you are *the people of God*; you had not received mercy, but now you have received mercy."[32] (Emphasis mine)

The church that Jesus said He would build and the gates of hell would not be able to prevail against, would be that nation, a holy nation, which would be granted the Kingdom of God on the earth and the keys to it. The church of Jesus would be composed of both Jew and Gentile, because He came to do away with those divisive terms. As Paul wrote, "There is neither Jew nor Greek (Gentile), there is neither slave nor free man, there is not male and female; for you are all one in Christ Jesus. And if you are Christ's, then you are Abraham's seed, heirs according to promise."[33] Jesus broke down the barrier wall between Jew and Gentile, reconciling both into one body, His body, His church, His new nation.[34]

And as that nation, the people for God's own possession, it is its primary function, duty and responsibility to proclaim the excellencies of its King and the good news (gospel) of His Kingdom. All the more reason for the church of Jesus to be one, and to speak and live as one, so that the whole world would know that Jesus is Savior, Lord and King, to the glory of Almighty God, our Abba Father.

End of Part Two. Respectfully submitted for your study, prayer and consideration. August 12, 2006.

The Gospel
Part Three

As members of the church of Jesus, the new nation, being representatives of the King and His Kingdom, how can we best proclaim the Gospel of the Kingdom of God? Perhaps it would be good for us to realize at this point that the King has appointed the people of His rule to a very special position in His Kingdom. This position is not restricted to just a few of His people, but on the contrary, to all of His subjects. He calls us, authorizes us, and ordains us to be His ambassadors.

Paul, an apostle, put it this way:

Therefore if anyone is in Christ, there is a new creation; the old things passed away; behold, new things have come. Now all things are from God, who reconciled us to Himself through Christ and gave us the ministry of reconciliation, namely, that God was in Christ reconciling the world to Himself, not counting their trespasses against them, and having committed to us the word of reconciliation. Therefore, we are ambassadors for Christ, as though God were making an appeal through us...be reconciled to God.[1]

How then should that message of reconciliation begin? What better way for it to begin than to follow the example of John, the baptizer, and

23

Jesus Himself, by proclaiming as they did, "Repent, for the Kingdom of God is at hand."[2] The proclamation of the Gospel of the Kingdom of God was the message authorized by Jesus to His twelve chosen apostles. [3] This was also the same message He authorized seventy other of His disciples to proclaim.[4] And it is precisely the same message which He authorizes all believers to proclaim today.[5] Therefore, what an excellent way for us to begin our ministry of reconciliation as ambassadors of Christ.

Not only did Jesus authorize the message to be proclaimed—that of the good news(Gospel) of the coming of the Kingdom of God—He authorized then, and continues to authorize today, His followers to perform miracles(signs and wonders) in His name by healing the sick, casting out demons or unclean spirits, raising the dead, cleansing lepers and others suffering from various diseases, causing the blind to see and the lame to walk—just as He had done in their presence and documented for us by the Holy Spirit in the Bible.[6] He also instructs His ambassadors to present the keys to the Kingdom of God by making disciples of all the nations, baptizing them in the name of the Father, Son and Holy Spirit, and teaching them in turn all the things He had taught and is still teaching today through His Word.[7]

The message of the Kingdom proclaimed and the miracles performed in the King's name open the door of opportunity to introduce people everywhere to the Lamb of God who, by His blood, took away the sins of the world, delivering those who would believe from the law of sin and death, and restoring their relationship with their Creator, Abba Father. This one who first appeared as the Suffering Servant, willing to lay down His own life for the sake of ours, is now and forever the King. Once this love of Abba Father and Jesus His Son is presented, there can only be one of two possible responses to the invitation to enter His Kingdom.

One response, sadly, would be the outright rejection of the invitation, the King Himself, and His Kingdom. Should one choose to respond in this way, and refuse His invitation to enter into and become a part of His Kingdom, what is the only possible reaction to be expected from the one who so loved them that He gave His only begotten Son as a ransom for them?[8] Jesus gives us the answer to the question in the form of another of His parables. He compared the Kingdom of heaven to a man who prepared a wedding feast for his son. He then sent out his servant, not once but twice, to gather together the invited guests, but they refused to come, giving one excuse after another. The host of the feast was angry at those who had rejected him and his invitation, and rescinded the invitation, leaving them to a fate worse than death. Instead, he instructed his servant to bring to his feast the poor, crippled, blind, and lame of the city, and even people from out in the highways and byways.[9]

The other possible response of course would be to gratefully accept such a gracious invitation. This response would be the same reaction as those who were gathered together on the day of Pentecost in Jerusalem. When confronted with the truth that their sins and actions had brought about the crucifixion of Jesus, the Son of God, the Lord Himself, their promised Messiah and King, they were beside themselves with remorse and cried out to Peter and the others, "Brothers, what shall we do?"[10] In answer to their question, rather than to bring justly deserved condemnation upon them, Peter offered instead the invitation of a lifetime. He presented them with the keys to the Kingdom of God:

> Repent, and each of you be baptized in the name of Jesus Christ for the forgiveness of your sins; and you will receive the gift of the Holy Spirit. For the promise is for you and your children and for all who are far off, as many as the Lord our God will call to Himself.[11]

When those keys to the Kingdom were presented by Peter on the feast day of Pentecost, some three thousand souls that very same day entered the Kingdom of God.[12]

Have you ever noticed that it was Peter, the apostle, who was given the privilege of being the first to present the keys to the Kingdom, not only there in Jerusalem, Judea, as we have just seen, but also to the

Samaritans[13], and even to the Gentiles at the house of Cornelius, a Roman centurion.[14] This should not be surprising at all. Was it not Jesus Himself who promised Peter, after he had received the revelation from Abba Father that Jesus was the Christ, the Son of the living God, "I will give you the keys of the Kingdom of Heaven; and whatever you bind on earth shall have been bound in Heaven, and whatever you loose on earth shall have been loosed in Heaven."[15]

The use of those keys to the Kingdom of God, however, were not in any way restricted to one man. They are the same keys which have been presented to and received by multitudes upon multitudes down through the years. Those who gladly received the invitation to enter the Kingdom of God have thereby been delivered from the kingdom of darkness and translated into the Kingdom of the Son of Abba Father's love.[16] Therefore, when presenting others with the Gospel of the Kingdom of God, and when confronted with the same question, "What shall I or we do?" we should immediately be prompted to use those very same keys to open the door of the Kingdom to them.

Is it possible that the message ordained by the Father, proclaimed by His Son, and taught by the apostles as they were moved by the Holy Spirit, has been diluted, watered down by the church of today? For some reason the emphasis is no longer placed on the fact that the Kingdom of God has come, and that we, if we truly desire to be citizens of it, must repent of our ways, choose to obey the King, and live according to the principles He has set forth for His Kingdom.

Perhaps it would be best at this point to give a brief definition of the Kingdom of God, as well as, a timeline for its existence. Simply stated, the Kingdom of God is the realm where Almighty God Himself rules and reigns as King and where His will is obeyed. Now, is that Kingdom past, present, or future? The answer to that question is, "Yes!" It is past, present, and future. The one true and living God is eternal, and so is His Kingdom. Abba Father has always existed, had no beginning, and has no end.[17] Even before He created the heavens and the earth, He existed. He is timeless. He created time, not for Himself, but for mankind. As

He spoke to Job, "Where were you when I laid the foundation of the earth?"[18]

The Bible begins with the words, "In the beginning God created the heavens and the earth."[19] Notice that the heavens are first in His order of creation. That means that the heavenly host, consisting of angels, archangels, seraphim, and cherubim were the inhabitants of that heavenly realm or Kingdom,[20] with God Himself being the King, the Lord of hosts, as declared in later times by the prophet Isaiah, who was privileged to see the King and His heavenly Kingdom in a vision.[21] So, even before the foundations of the earth were laid, the King and His Kingdom existed.

Did the Kingdom of God exist on the earth before the coming of Jesus? Yes. When Almighty God first created man and woman, He instructed them to be fruitful and multiply, filling the earth with children, granting them full authority to subdue and rule over the earth.[22] He was establishing His Kingdom on the earth. He was the King, and Adam and Eve and their progeny were to be the subjects of His Kingdom on the earth. God provided all their needs—food in abundance, access to the fruit of the tree of life, itself, which would allow them to live forever, and personal and intimate fellowship with His subjects.[23] An ideal life in a perfect Kingdom with God Himself as their King!

Remember, however, that in our definition of the Kingdom of God we said that the King not only rules but is obeyed. There was only one commandment set forth by the King for His subjects to obey in order for this perfect paradise to continue forever. While the fruit of the tree of life was accessible to them, as were all the other fruit-bearing trees, the subjects in the Kingdom were specifically told not to eat of the fruit of the tree of the knowledge of good and evil.[24] Disobedience to the King would be costly. The beautiful Kingdom garden given them to share would be taken away. No longer would they have access to eternal life. And worst of all that daily, intimate and personal relationship with the King would come to an end.[25] And, so it came to pass. Disobey they did, and judgment by the King was swift.

Seemingly, mankind was on its own. Oh, the King was still King, but His earthly people were now subject to the law of sin and death. They had been created to live forever and in perfect health. But disobedience brought about sickness and death. The King had said to Adam, "From any tree of the garden you may eat freely, but from the tree of the knowledge of good and evil you may not eat from it, for in the day that you eat from it you will surely die."[26] And in the day of their rebellion they did begin to die, both physically and spiritually. They died spiritually, immediately, as the King drove them out of His garden and out of His presence.[27]

But did they die physically the very day of their disobedience? It would seem not since Adam lived for nine hundred and thirty years; and Jared lived for nine hundred and sixty-two years; and Methuselah, the oldest of the King's subjects, lived nine hundred and sixty-nine years.[28] Remember, however, that time was created by the King for man and not for Himself, and as Peter, the apostle, tells us, "But do not let this escape your notice, beloved, that with the Lord(King) one day is like a thousand years, and a thousand years like one day."[29] Now notice that no one lived on the earth longer than Methuselah!

Permit me to interject here a personal observation that has fascinated me for some time. The father of Methuselah was Enoch, and we are told that he only lived on the earth for three hundred and sixty-five years. In tracing the generations of Adam in the fifth chapter of the Book of Genesis, one can discern that Adam was still alive during the life of Enoch. Imagine with me, if you will, that Enoch had the opportunity to visit his great(times four!) grandfather Adam, perhaps on numerous occasions, and on those occasions it would not seem implausible for Enoch to ask Adam to tell him again and again what life was like in the Garden of Eden, and what joy he must have known to be able to walk with the King Himself in that garden. Enoch must have had a thousand questions for Adam![30] What makes me think so? Because it must have been the desire of Enoch's heart to have that kind of personal relationship with the King. We are told that "Enoch walked with God; and he was not, for God took him."[31] Enoch did not die. He was, in a moment, in the twinkling of an eye, with the King!

What had happened to the Kingdom of God on the earth in the meanwhile? It had become corrupt to the core. So much so that the King saw the wickedness of man, read the continual evil thoughts of his heart, and regretted that He had ever created him and all the living things on the earth, and so planned to blot them all out.[32] And so He did, with one main exception. There was a man, perhaps somewhat like Enoch, who was righteous in the sight of the King and who found favor in His sight. His name was Noah. He, his wife, their three sons, their spouses, and animals and birds as ordained by the King were saved from the overwhelming flood which covered the earth. The King preserved the remnant of His Kingdom on earth because one man found favor in His sight and obeyed Him. A covenant was established between the King and the remnant of His Kingdom that He would never again destroy the earth and everything in it by flood waters. To this day, the sign of that covenant can be seen during or following a rain storm—the rainbow.[33]

From the families of the sons of Noah came the nations of the world; and while it was the intention of the King for these nations to spread out and populate the entire earth, disobedience once more attempted to confound the King's purposes. Those nations, all speaking the same language, determined to build a city for themselves with a tower reaching into Heaven itself, because they did not desire to be scattered all over the earth. But the King, together with His Son and Holy Spirit, once more invaded the earth, confused their language by turning their communication with one another into mere babble, and scattered them over the face of the whole earth.[34]

It is interesting to note that on another occasion there would be a similar invasion of the earth by the Heavenly Threesome. On the fulfillment of the Day of Pentecost, as was promised by the King, Abba Father would send His Holy Spirit to the King's subjects, and they would all begin to speak with other languages or tongues. Unlike at the Tower

29

of Babel, this time, these different languages would be designed to unite the people, as each would be able to understand in their own language or dialect the messages being conveyed.[35] And what joyous messages they would be, all about the King and the coming to earth once again of His Kingdom. But I am getting ahead of myself!

Once the nations were scattered over the earth, the King desired to create one great nation which would prove to be a blessing to all the families of the earth. For this task He chose a seventy-five year old man named Abram as His anointed one. The King took him to Canaan and promised to give this land to his descendants.[36] At this point Abram had no descendants of his own, but some twenty-four years later, the King promised Abram that he would become not only an exalted father(the meaning of the name Abram), but also the father of a multitude of nations(the meaning of his new name, Abraham).[37]

Through Abraham and his descendants (seed) God established a covenant whereby once again His Kingdom would be on the earth, and He would be the King, and they would be His subjects.[38] One year later, to the surprise and delight of Sarah, now ninety years of age, she gave birth to a son, Isaac.[39] This was the beginning of the fulfillment of the promise to Abraham that through him and his seed to follow the nations of the earth would be blessed.[40] Prior to this, of course, plans of man, in this case Sarai and Abram, in their effort to help God along with His plan, tried to come up with their own solutions, and so resulted in the birth of Ishmael through Hagar, Sarai's maid.[41] But that is another matter not applicable to our present endeavor. Suffice it to say that the King is quite capable of causing His will to be accomplished regardless of the confusion and chaos instigated by man![42]

The establishment of God's Kingdom on the earth passed from Abraham to Isaac and his bride, Rebekah, who received the blessing of her family in these words, "May you, our sister, become thousands of ten thousands, and may your seed possess the gate of those who hate them."[43] From Isaac and Rebekah the Kingdom passed to Jacob and not Esau as ordained by the King.[44] The King appeared to Jacob, changing his name to Israel and instructing him with these words, "I AM El Shaddai(God Almighty); be fruitful and multiply; a nation and a company of nations shall come into being from you, and kings shall come forth from your loins. The land which I gave to Abraham and Isaac, I will give it to you, and I will give the land to your seed after you."[45] The seed to whom the Kingdom passed were the twelve sons of Jacob who later composed the nation of Israel.

Much, of course, had to happen in the interim before the nation of Israel could become full blown. Jealousy and downright hatred reared their ugly heads against Joseph, the son of Rachel, by his brothers who sold him as a slave and caused him to wind up in Egypt.[46] But this too was all in the plan of the King for the ultimate placing of His Kingdom in the land of Canaan as He had promised Abraham.[47] Before that would occur, the Kingdom of God on earth would reside in Egypt at first as a great nation there.[48] After Joseph's death, there followed for the Kingdom of the sons of Israel four hundred years of slavery and oppression—just as the King had prophesied to Abram.[49]

As those four hundred years were coming to a close, the King raised up another leader for His Kingdom who would ultimately lead His people out of the land of bondage and into the land flowing with milk and honey, Canaan. Born to parents from the tribe of Levi, hidden from the authorities in Egypt so as not to be killed, set afloat by his mother among the reeds of the Nile River, discovered by the daughter of Pharaoh, reared by her to manhood in Pharaoh's palace, fleeing from the wrath of Pharaoh after killing an Egyptian for beating one of his brother Hebrew slaves, living for years as a shepherd in Midian, coming into the very presence of God the King at Mount Horeb, Moses was anointed by the King to deliver the sons of Israel from their long years of bondage.[50]

It is one thing to be chosen and anointed for the purposes of God the King. It is quite another to overcome fear and trepidation in the carrying out of those purposes. So it was for Moses. Without the presence, power, and authority of the King Himself, Moses' tasks would not have been possible—nor would he have been able to overcome his fears. But the King was with him, and although he had to endure doubt of his own, rejection by not only Pharaoh but his own Hebrew brethren, deliverance from slavery in Egypt at the hand of the King became a reality for the citizens of the Kingdom of God, and they feared, revered, and believed in their King and in the servant of the King, Moses.[51] At least for the moment!

When water was bitter and food was not to be found, there was murmuring and complaining by the citizens of the Kingdom directed at Moses, but in reality against their King. And, each time the King provided for them in abundance. For example, He fed them bread from Heaven(manna) for forty years on their way to Canaan.[52] When the manna did not seem to be enough, they cried out in protest and greed for meat, and the King provided them with quail, a whole month's supply of quail, until they had so much quail that it came out their noses and made them sick![53] Perhaps there is a message here for the King's kids of today!

What was the King's plan for His people after He had delivered them out of the hands of their oppressors? He revealed it to them in these words delivered by His servant Moses, "You yourselves have seen what I did to the Egyptians, and I bore you on eagles' wings, and brought you to Myself. Now then, if you will indeed obey My voice and keep My covenant, then you shall be My own possession(or special treasure) among all the peoples, for all the earth is Mine; and you shall be to Me a *Kingdom of priests and a holy nation.*"[54] That was His plan and purpose. Notice that the King's plan was conditional on their obedience to His voice and His covenant. And what was His covenant to which they all agreed to follow?[55] It was the Constitution, so to speak, of the Kingdom, the Preamble to which I have taken the liberty to present in brief form and in my own words as follows:

> There is only one God and He is your King. Don't try to have another or set up an idol of one to worship. Keep the King's commandments.

Don't speak evil of Him. Man and beast alike, do your work in six days and rest on the seventh, keeping it holy. Bring honor to your Dad and Mom. No murder. No adultery. No stealing. No speaking evil of your neighbor. No jealousy or desiring what is not yours, but rather be content with what the King has provided you.[56]

Thousands of years later and in a more succinct and far more powerful way than my attempt, the Preamble to the Constitution was presented in these words, "You shall love the Lord your God with all your heart, and with all your soul, and with all your mind." And, "You shall love your neighbor as yourself."[57]

When Moses presented the whole Constitution of the Kingdom of God to the people, they, with one voice, promised to do the King's will and be obedient.[58] But did they? No. Within days after Moses ascended Mount Sinai to receive the Constitution in stone, the people did the very thing the King told them not to do; they sought out a god of their own making—a golden calf. The King in His anger decided to destroy them and instead establish His Kingdom through Moses. What an honor for one man to hear! But Moses instead entreated the King to spare the people, and the King relented.[59] Instead, the King agreed to continue leading His subjects, working through Moses alone as His spokesman, speaking to him face to face and appearing in a cloud by day and fire by night to His subjects.[60]

The time came when the King was ready for His subjects to enter into the land of promise—the new country for His Kingdom. He instructed Moses to send representatives from the twelve tribes of Israel to spy out their intended new home which He promised to give them. The twelve returned with praises for the magnificent fruit of the land—a land which truly flowed with milk and honey. However, ten of the twelve spies, out of fear and rebellion, persuaded the people not to go in and take the land. Only Caleb and Joshua were willing and anxious to be obedient to the King. Again the King was determined to do away with the people and create a Kingdom in and through Moses. But again Moses interceded on behalf of the people, and again the King relented, but only under the condition that all those over the age of twenty, with the exception of Caleb and Joshua, would not be able to enter into the land that the King was providing for them.[61]

Because of their continual rebellion, it would be forty years before the King would allow His subjects to enter into Canaan.[62] Not even Moses was allowed to enter into the promised land because of his own disobedience. Instead, the King appointed Joshua to lead His people into their new home.[63] And so, the adventures and battles in taking the land followed, the King being with them to fight for them against their enemies.[64] The land ultimately was taken and divided among the twelve tribes of Israel, and the Kingdom of God now consisted of the boundaries set forth by the King.[65] Joshua had proven to be a faithful servant of the King.

Following the death of Joshua, there arose a generation who no longer knew the King and all that He had done for them. They did evil in the sight of the King by serving false gods. So, the King allowed the enemies of Israel to overcome them. When they were deeply distressed and cried out to the King, He appointed over them judges to lead them and deliver them from their enemies; the first such judge being Othniel, the younger brother of Caleb.[66] There followed a series of judges ordained by the King, and a pattern developed. When the people of His Kingdom were disobedient to Kingdom principles, the neighboring nations would overcome them. When they cried out for deliverance, the King would raise up another judge to lead them. And so it went, rejecting the King and His ways and suffering the consequences by being ruled by their enemies; crying out to the King and being supplied with another judge who would deliver them.[67] After the time of the Judges there arose a time when there was no leader for the Kingdom of God on the earth. Rather than hearken to their King, "everyone did what was right in his own eyes."[68]

Following these times, the King raised up and confirmed for Himself a prophet by the name of Samuel to judge His people. And Samuel served the King in that ministry all his life. When he was old, he tried to appoint his sons as judges, but they were dishonest—not like Samuel at all—and were rejected by the people who now demanded that Samuel appoint for them a flesh and blood king to judge them, similar to the kings of all the other nations around them. Being grieved, Samuel prayed to the King who assured him that he was not the one being rejected, but that He, their true King, was being rejected by them. Even in their rebellion against Him, the King provided for them an earthly king to reign over them.[69]

Making certain that the people fully understood the consequences of their demand, the King set forth the customs of kings who would rule over them. They would be subjected to giving their sons and daughters to forced labor, their sons to military draft the seizure of the best of their lands and cattle, paying taxes, and more burdens. But the people continued to demand an earthly king to be appointed over them.[70] There is a valuable lesson to be learned here. Be careful of what you demand, desire, and that for which you pray. You may get what you ask for! Little did they know what they were bargaining for when they were willing to give up their heavenly King for an earthly one. Yet, as would soon be seen, the King of Heaven would still very much be in total control of His Kingdom on earth.

The tall, handsome Saul was chosen by the King to serve as prince(their earthy king) over His Kingdom of Israel.[71] Samuel anointed Saul who then received the anointing of the King Himself by the Holy Spirit coming upon him. The King performed on Saul what may have been the very first heart transplant! The people of the Kingdom acknowledged Saul as their king.[72] All this time the true King gave directions to Saul, the surrogate king, through His servant Samuel. And it is in this regard that Saul failed the true King. First of all, he was instructed to wait for Samuel at Gilgal for seven days, when the prophet was to come and offer up offerings and sacrifices to the King prior to the battle against the Philistines. When the prophet did not appear in the time that Saul thought he should, he decided to offer up the sacrifices to the King himself.[73] Later, he was given strict instructions as to how to deal with the Amalekites. Saul failed, again, to carry out all the details of the task set before him. As a result of his disobedience, he was removed as king of the Kingdom of God by the King.[74]

In Saul's place the King chose David, a man from Bethlehem—the youngest son of Jesse—to be their new king. Once anointed, the Holy Spirit came upon David and departed from Saul.[75] The King declared that the house of David and the Kingdom over which He had appointed him would endure forever—that the throne of David would be established forever.[76] David was a mighty warriors delivering the Kingdom of Israel from Goliath and his fellow Philistines, as well as, all the enemies of the Kingdom. The King protected David and raised him up in the sight of all the people. And, even though David sinned greatly before the King by coveting another man's wife, committing adultery with her, and murdering her husband, when confronted by the prophet of God, repented and declared that it was God the King he had sinned against, and the King spared his life. He, however, would pay dearly for his transgressions.[77]

Just prior to his death, David ordered, as he had promised, that Solomon be anointed king over the Kingdom in his stead.[78] When asked by the King what he would have Him give him, Solomon requested a hearing heart to be able to judge properly the citizens of the Kingdom. The King was so pleased with Solomon's answer that He gave him, in addition to the gifts of wisdom and discernment, great riches, honor and long life, as long as he walked according to Kingdom principles. [79] And, as the King had promised, it would be Solomon, the son of David, who was granted the privilege of building the Temple for the true King.[80] After it was built, the King gave a stern warning to Solomon and all who would succeed him, that if he or they would not follow the King and keep the commandments and statutes of the Kingdom, the citizens of the Kingdom would be cut off and the Temple would wind up as a heap of ruins.[81]

Sadly, even Solomon turned away from the ways of the King, and following Solomon, successors to the throne of the Kingdom arose—most of whom also did not follow the ways of the King. The Temple, itself, would be destroyed by the Babylonians. Years later, just as Jesus had prophesied to His disciples, the Temple would be totally and completely destroyed.[82]

Following Solomon's reign the King divided His Kingdom—ten tribes of Israel under Jeroboam and two tribes of Judah under Rehoboam. From this point on, with but few exceptions, those chosen to lead the King's people did not follow in the ways of the true King. The people of the Kingdom suffered thereby, their leaders turning to quests for personal power and idolatry.[83] There were a few kings who did right in the sight of the King, such as Asa, Jehoshaphat, Jehoash, Hezekiah, and especially, Josiah.[84]

But the time finally came when the King had had enough and turned His Kingdom over to a foreign ruler, declaring him to be king over His people. He was Nebuchadnezzar, king of Babylon, ending the reigns of Hebrew kings over Israel and Judah, at least until the coming of the King of all kings, Jesus. There would be a time in the interim for the rebuilding of the Temple in Jerusalem with the approval of Cyrus, the king of Persia. But this would take several years during the time of the ministries of the leaders chosen, Ezra and Nehemiah,[85] by the King.

All during the times of the kings and leaders of the Kingdom of God, the King was very much in control of His Kingdom. Time and again He spoke through His prophets to His people, encouraging them to follow in His path and warning them of the consequences of their failure to do so.[86] The era of the existence of the Kingdom of God in the past came to a close with the words of the prophet Malachi, giving the final admonition from the King to all the people of the earth, who in fact and in truth make up His Kingdom on the earth. Consider carefully the warnings and the promises of the King:

For behold, the day is coming, burning like a furnace; and all the arrogant and every evildoer will be chaff, and the day that is coming will set them ablaze," says the Lord of hosts, "so that it will leave them neither root nor branch. But for you who fear My name, the sun of righteousness will rise with healing in its wings; and you will go forth and skip about like calves from the stall. You will tread down the wicked, for they will be ashes under the soles of your feet on the day which I am preparing," says the Lord of hosts. "Remember the law of Moses My servant, statutes and ordinances which I commanded him in Horeb for all Israel. Behold, I am going to send you Elijah the prophet before the coming of the great and terrible day of the Lord. He will restore or turn the hearts of the fathers to children and the hearts of the children to their fathers so that I will not come and smite the land with a curse.[87]

Following this admonition there is a period of some four hundred years of seemingly complete silence from the King to His people. But rest assured, during those years the King was still in residence, and His Kingdom principles still in effect. Concerning the subject of the Kingdom of God in the past, this has been but a thumbnail sketch of its past history. And this brings us back to the Kingdom of God of the present when Jesus first came in human form to the earth—as discussed in Parts One and Two of this treatise. We will attempt to continue the subject of the present day Kingdom of God from the days of Jesus to the days in which we now live. But prior to that, we will turn our attention next in Part Four to the Kingdom of God future.

End of Part Three. Respectfully submitted for your study, prayer and consideration. October 30, 2006.

The Gospel
Part Four

The psalmist declared, "Your Kingdom is a Kingdom of all ages, and Your dominion throughout all generations."[1] The King is eternal. So, too, is His Kingdom. We have tasted a bit of the Kingdom past, and to a degree, the Kingdom present. For now, permit me to share a few glimpses of the Kingdom future. The King in His Word has revealed a day in which His Kingdom will be the only Kingdom on the face of the earth. All other kingdoms, together with their kings, will be done away.[2] At that time the words of the psalmist when he wrote, "For the Kingdom is the Lord's, and He rules over the nations,"[3] will be fully made manifest. Oh, to be sure, the King already rules over all nations, but most of those nations, if not all, are not even aware of that fact!

The psalmist has a message for all the nations of the world and all the inhabitants of those nations. He wrote, "The earth is the Lord's, and all its fullness, the world and those who dwell in it."[4] One day, when those who have heard the Gospel of the Kingdom of God and have rendered obedience to the King, they will accompany Him as He approaches the very gates of heaven and will be able to shout with joy to the gate keepers, "Lift up your heads, O gates, and be lifted up, O everlasting doors, that the King of glory may come in!" And when the gate keeper

39

wants to know who it is that is knocking at the door of Heaven, the chorus will ring out, "The Lord strong and mighty, the Lord mighty in battle… the Lord of hosts, He is the King of glory!"[5]

The Kingdom of God future has been described in many ways throughout the pages of Scripture. It will not be possible to cover them all in this treatise, but we would be remiss if we were not to share a few of the highlights. If you were asked about the Kingdom of God in the future, what would be your response? Many would no doubt assume that you must be referring to the time when the world is destroyed, and believers will be in Heaven with the King. But do the Scriptures bear this out?

For example, what did Jesus mean in His Preamble to the Constitution when He said, "Blessed are the gentle (or humble, or meek), for they shall inherit the earth."[6] Notice that He did not say that they would inherit Heaven. Rather, He was referring to the time when they, the meek, would be ruling with Him on earth. And, when will that take place? It will occur when He comes again, this time to rule and reign in person on the earth. How can we know this to be true? Hear it from the King Himself:

> But when the Son of Man comes (to earth) in His glory, and all the angels with Him, then He will sit on His glorious throne. All the nations will be gathered before Him; and He will separate them from one another, as the shepherd separates the sheep from the goats; and He will put the sheep on His right, and the goats on His left. Then the King will say to those on His right, "Come, you who are blessed of My Father, inherit the Kingdom prepared for you from the foundation of the world."[7]

What exactly will be this Kingdom to which the King referred? Will it not be the very Kingdom on the earth for which He taught us to pray, "Your Kingdom come. Your will be done, on earth as it is in heaven."[8] When the King comes again, Heaven itself will be opened, and the King of kings and Lord of lords, riding a white horse, will be revealed; and He will come to rule or shepherd the nations with a rod of iron and the sword of His Word.[9] During this time the King will bind Satan and throw him into the abyss for a period of one thousand years, and he will no longer be able to deceive the people of the world for all those years. And the saints, holy ones of God, the faithful believers in the King and His Kingdom will reign with Him on the earth for those one thousand years.[10]

This will include those faithful who had died before His coming again, as well as those who are still alive at His coming. Concerning those who have died before the King's coming again, Paul, an apostle of the King, reassures us that when the King comes, He will bring with Him all those who previously died in Him. They will be the first to rise from the dead and will accompany Him. Then, those saints who are still alive when He comes will rise and join them to greet the King as He assumes His throne.[11] What will be the experience at that time for those believers who are still alive when the King comes? Again, hear the words of Paul concerning this matter:

> Now I say this, brethren, that flesh and blood cannot inherit the Kingdom of God (future), nor does corruption inherit incorruption. Behold, I tell you a mystery; we will not all sleep, but we will be changed, in a moment, in the twinkling of an eye, at the last trumpet; for the trumpet will sound, and the dead will be raised incorruptible, and we will be changed. For this corruptible must put on incorruption, and this mortal must put on immortality. But when this corruptible will have put on immortality, then will come about the saying that is written, "Death is swallowed up in victory. O death, where is your victory? O death where is your sting? The sting of death is sin, and the power of sin is the law; but thanks be to God who gives us the victory through our Lord (and King) Jesus."[12]

How will all this come about, and what will life be like in the Kingdom of God future here on the earth? First things first. The coming again of the King is described for us in several places in Scripture. When

41

King Jesus ascended into Heaven to be with Abba Father after spending forty days with His disciples speaking of the things concerning the Kingdom of God, they, His disciples, kept watching as He disappeared from their sight. Messengers of the King, dressed in white clothing, made an astounding statement: "This Jesus, who has been taken up from you into Heaven, will come in just the same way as you have watched Him go into Heaven."[13] What a day that will be! His coming is described for us by the prophet Zechariah:

> In that day His feet will stand on the Mount of Olives which is in front of Jerusalem on the east—exactly from where He had ascended—and the Mount of Olives will be split in the middle from east to west by a very large valley, so that half of the mountain will move toward the north and the other half toward the south…Then the Lord, my God (the King), will come, and all the holy ones with Him!…And the Lord will be King over all the earth.[14]

See it through the eyes of Daniel who was blessed with a dream and visions of the coming of the King and His Kingdom future. He wrote, "I kept looking in the night visions, and behold, with the clouds of heaven one like a Son of Man was coming, and He came up to the Ancient of Days and was presented before Him. And to Him was given dominion, glory, and a Kingdom that all the peoples, nations and tongues might serve Him. His dominion is an everlasting dominion which will not pass away; and His Kingdom is one which will not be destroyed."[15]

Can one even begin to imagine such a scene! And yet, we are told that the whole world will be witnesses to it. "Behold, He is coming with the clouds, and every eye will see Him, even those who pierced Him; and all the tribes of the earth will mourn over Him. So it is to be. Amen."[16] In years past many have wondered how it would be possible for the whole world to witness this spectacle, but not so today in this age when we can literally, instantly and simultaneously see what is happening throughout the four corners of the earth by way of our satellite systems.

What will life be like in the Kingdom of God on the earth when the King is in residence in Jerusalem? We can catch a glimpse of this time when we review a familiar passage of Scripture, "And the government (Kingdom) will be on His shoulders; and His name will be called Wonderful Counselor, Mighty God, Eternal Father, Prince of Peace. There will be no end to the increase of His government or of peace, on the throne of David and over His Kingdom, to establish it and to uphold it with justice and righteousness from then on and forevermore. The zeal of the Lord of hosts will accomplish this."[17]

What of the citizens of His Kingdom future? How is life described for them? They will be given the privilege of ruling and reigning with Him over all the nations and kingdoms of the earth. Listen, again, to the revelation given to Daniel: "Then the Kingdom, the dominion, and the greatness of the kingdoms under the whole heaven will be given to the people of the holy ones (saints) of the Highest One (the King); His Kingdom an everlasting Kingdom, and all the dominions will serve and obey Him (the King)."[18] Serving the King by ministering to Him and, by His authority ministering to the peoples of the world, will be the function of Kingdom future citizens.

In those days, when the citizens of the Kingdom future are abiding with their King without any interference from Satan, now securely bound by the King in the abyss, life on this earth will be much different in many ways than life as we know it today. The prophet Isaiah, by revelation from the throne of God, described life as it will be in Kingdom future. Consider some of the following:

We see, for example, that Jerusalem will be the epicenter of the whole world. Peoples from all the nations will travel to Mount Zion to be taught firsthand from the King Himself. There will be one law—His law—which will come forth from His throne. By that law the King will be the Judge handing down His decisions affecting all the nations and peoples then on the earth. War will be no more, for every nation will abide by the rulings of the King.[19] Those rulings are further described in these words, "With righteousness He will judge the poor, and decide with fairness for the afflicted of the earth; and He will strike the earth with the rod of His mouth, and with the breath of His lips He will slay the wicked. Also righteousness will be the belt about His loins, and faithfulness the belt about His waist."[20] Finally, the rule and reign of a truly benevolent King over all the earth!

Do you recall that following Solomon's reign the King divided His Kingdom in two—ten tribes of Israel and two tribes of Judah. There will no longer be division in the Kingdom of God future. Not only will all Israel be united, but all Israel and the other nations will be united under the King, for the King will be King over all the earth.[21] As an example of this the prophet speaks of a highway from Egypt to Assyria (Assyria includes the present day nations of Syria, Lebanon, Jordan, and northern Iraq), right through Israel. The three will worship together and be a blessing for the whole world to see.[22] This highway will be called the Highway of Holiness leading to Mount Zion; upon this highway only the redeemed, the saints or holy ones of the King will be allowed to travel and in complete safety.[23]

Animal life will be different in the Kingdom of God future. Whereas now a lamb is prey for the wolf, the goat is prey for the leopard, and the calf is prey for the lion, such will not be the case in His Kingdom. They, as well as the cow, the ox and the bear will all graze together on straw, and little children will be able to lead not only the cattle but the former carnivorous beasts as well. Once poisonous, snakes will no longer bite or harm anyone, especially small babies. The peace and tranquility of the King will be known even by the animal world.[24]

No longer will the Jews be despised by peoples of other nations. Instead, many of those very nations will now serve the chosen people of the King, because His light and glory will arise upon them. Any nation refusing to serve the King and His people will be brought to ruin.[25] In the Kingdom of God future who will be the true chosen people of the King? They will consist of not only the remnant of the twelve tribes of Israel, but also all those who wear the robe of righteousness, the Robe of the King, those who are sons and daughters of Abraham, both by natural birth and those who have been adopted. Consider these words of the prophet Zechariah, "'Sing for joy and be glad, O daughter of Zion; for behold I am coming and I will dwell in your midst,' declares the Lord (King). 'Many nations will join themselves to the Lord (King) in that day and will become My people. Then I will dwell in your midst, and you will know that the Lord of hosts has sent Me to you.'"[26] In other words, all those who are a part of the body of Christ, Jew and Gentile alike, made one by the King Himself.[27]

The average life of the citizen of the Kingdom of God future will be much longer on the earth than it is at the present time. No more infant deaths. Young people will live to be at least one hundred, and if they should die before then they will be considered cursed. Old men will fill out their days in peace, safety, and prosperity and not have to give their children for war or calamity. All of this will take place in the new earth created by the King.[28]

In the Kingdom of God future the Dead Sea will no longer be dead. Water will flow from the Temple in Jerusalem down into the Dead Sea, and it will become alive and fresh, for it too will empty into the sea. Where now nothing can live in the Dead Sea, then the sea will be teeming with fish of all kinds, shapes, and sizes. The salt from the Dead Sea, including all the minerals, will still be available in the swamps and marshes nearby. On both sides of the river flowing into and out of the Dead Sea there will be fruit-bearing trees twelve months out of the year—the fruit from which will provide food for the citizens of the Kingdom, and the leaves of which will be used for healing purposes.[29]

What is this Temple in Jerusalem from which the water will flow? It is the Temple of the King which will be built by His divine authority, in which will be His throne, and from which He will govern as both King and Priest.[30] The specific details of the construction of that Temple can be found in the pages of Ezekiel, chapters 40 through 44. As can be seen by the description of the Temple in Ezekiel, this is a Temple which has never before been built, but will be the Temple from which the King will rule during His one thousand year reign. There is, of course, a Temple of the King which is in existence today. No, it is not the ruins left behind on the Temple Mount upon which now sits the Dome of the Rock. Rather, it is the Temple described in these words of Paul, the apostle, "Do you not know that you (fellow bondservants of the Christ) are a Temple of God, and the Spirit of God dwells in you?" And he also wrote, "Or do you (again, fellow bondservants of the Lord) not know that your body is a Temple of the Holy Spirit who is in you, whom you have from God, and that you are not your own? For you have been bought with a price: therefore glorify God in your body."[31] Peter speaks of this Temple in these words, "...you also, as living stones, are being built up as a spiritual house for a holy priesthood, to offer up spiritual sacrifices acceptable to God through Jesus Christ.[32] Even so, though the body of Christ is a spiritual Temple of the Lord today, there will yet be built a physical Temple for the King and His Kingdom of God future.

The pages of the Old Testament or Covenant (of which just a few have been included in this writing), in describing the Kingdom of God future end by assuring us that the King will reign over all the earth, and that Jerusalem will dwell in peace and security. Everyone will know the King, and even the bells on the horses and simple cooking utensils will be clearly marked *Holy to the Lord*.[33]

Following the thousand year reign of the King in His Temple in Jerusalem, there will be yet another Kingdom of God future which is beautifully described by the King to His beloved John, that disciple whom He loved and who was part of His inner circle.[34] Any attempt on my part to describe it in my own words would be an act of utter futility. Therefore, I urge you to pause right now before proceeding any further and read it for yourself as it is written in the Book of Revelation.[35]

Before proceeding to comment on some of the things found in the above description of the final Kingdom of God future, I believe it would be fruitful for us to carefully consider the following words from the pen of the apostle Paul, because in a most important way it impacts on the Revelation account of that final Kingdom. Forgive me for interjecting my thoughts (in italics and in parentheses) in the middle of what the apostle wrote, but I believe it will clarify some important facts.

> But now Christ has been raised from the dead, the first fruits of those who are asleep. For since by a man (Adam) came death, by a man also (Jesus) *came* the resurrection of the dead. For as in Adam all die, so also in Christ (Messiah, King Jesus) all will be made alive. But each in his own order: Christ (the King) the first fruits, after that those who are Christ's at His coming, (*Please note that between this comma and the next word "then" there will have elapsed a period of one thousand years, the millennial reign of King Jesus!*) then *comes* the end, when He (King Jesus) hands over the Kingdom to the God and Father, when He (King Jesus) has abolished all rule and all authority and power. For He (King Jesus) must reign until He (Father God) has put all His enemies under His feet. (*For an in-depth consideration of the Father putting the enemies of the Son under the Son's feet, see the many Scriptures noted in footnote.*[36] The last enemy that will be abolished is death. For He (Father God) has put all things in subjection under His (King Jesus') feet. But when He (Father God) says, "All things are put in subjection," it is evident that He (Father God) is excepted who put all things in subjection to Him (King Jesus). When all things are subjected to Him (King Jesus), then the Son (King Jesus) Himself also will be subjected to the One (Father God) who subjected all things to Him (King Jesus), that God may be all in all.[37]

Now, in closing Part Four of this treatise, I would like to draw your attention to a few things in the Revelation description of the Kingdom of God future. First, please notice that the new Jerusalem comes down from the new heaven to the new earth, and it is here, in that new earth, where Father God will dwell with the people of His ultimate Kingdom future.[38] Next, note that only those who have been written in the Lamb's book of life will be allowed to dwell therein.[39] And it is here on this new earth that indeed there will be everlasting life. How can we know? Because the King's bride will have access to the tree of life once again![(40)] And it is also here that the King's bondservants will not only be able to serve Him personally, but they will be able to see the face of Father God and live![(41)] Finally, in the interim, so that the thousand year reign of King Jesus can begin, there is an admonition to prepare for His coming, for He says He will come quickly, and His reward with Him; and so for us to wash our robes to make certain that only righteousness can be seen in the lives of the citizens of the Kingdom of God.[(42)]

Let the cry of the redeemed of the earth be, "Amen! Come, King Jesus! "

End of Part Four. Respectfully submitted for your study, prayer and consideration. November 10, 2006.

The Gospel
Part Five

After such a delightful taste of what the Kingdom of God will be one day, it may be difficult for us to come back from the future! However, there is much still to share about the Kingdom of God present in order that we may better appreciate what is yet to come. While looking forward to that final Kingdom of God, permit me to share my thoughts concerning a very special song written by Himmie Gastafson, "I Hear a Sound Coming From the Mountain" (Copyright 1976, Integrity Hosanna Music). I sang this song often in the early years of my rescue from the kingdom of darkness into the Kingdom of the Son of His love. The song speaks of hearing a special sound coming from a mountain. The sound becomes clearer and more compelling from day to day. The King is on the top of that mountain, and He beckons to all with a voice so appealing that it seems as though all other sounds are hushed, and His message alone is all that matters. The message? "Prepare ye the way of the Lord."

Several years ago the Lord gave me another verse to this song. It goes this way: "Let us prepare to go up to the mountain. Let us prepare to ascend. Let us prepare to go up to the mountain, to worship our Lord and our King. To worship our Lord. To worship our King. To be with

49

our Lord and our King." The operative word, of course, is *prepare*. And so, as we return to the subject of the Kingdom of God present, may we focus on how best to prepare and be prepared for living in His Kingdom. This is a vital part of the Gospel of the Kingdom of God. The King has shown us the way.

The King emphasized that He had not come to do away with either the law or the prophets, but rather to fulfill them. He insisted that until the heaven and earth that we know today passes away and makes room for the new heavens and the new earth, no part of the law will be removed; and He admonished us not to annul one of His Father's commandments, because how we treated those commandments will greatly affect our standing in His Kingdom; and unless we were more righteous than the religious leaders of the day, we would not even be able to enter His Kingdom. [1]

Of all the commandments to be considered, the King was asked by a scribe or lawyer which were the most important of all. He answered by saying, "The first (and foremost) is, 'Hear, O Israel! The Lord our God is one Lord; and you shall love the Lord your God with all your heart, and with all your soul, and with all your mind, and with all your strength.' The second is this, 'You shall love your neighbor as yourself.' There is no other commandment greater than these." As a matter of fact, the lawyer was told that on these two commandments all of the law and prophets depend. The lawyer was delighted with the King's response and was told by the King that he himself was not far from the Kingdom of God. [2]

How important is it to obey the commandments of the King and His Father? Jesus made it very clear that merely calling Him "Lord" would not be sufficient. He put it this way, "Not everyone who says to Me, 'Lord, Lord,' will enter the Kingdom of heaven, but he who does the will of My Father who is in heaven." And the fact that they were able to cast out demons and perform miracles in His name would not necessarily prove that they were in His Kingdom. The true test would be whether or not they had an intimate relationship with the King, and more importantly, whether or not the King knew them intimately. The entrance to His Kingdom, He said, would be narrow, and few would be willing to seek out His way to life and follow it.[3]

Lest we draw the conclusion from the above that the casting out of demons is not authorized Kingdom activity, we need to remember that the Pharisees accused the King of casting out demons by the ruler of demons. He was quick to set them straight on two accounts. First, He made it clear that if He cast out demons by the finger of God, then it proved that the Kingdom of God had come upon them. Not only that, but He affirmed the fact that His disciples, their own sons, were also casting out demons by the power and authority of the Father of Heaven.[4] All of this plus the fact that the King Himself authorized His disciples then, and authorizes them now, to cast out demons.[5]

But what of the words of Jesus which seem to put down those who claimed to prophesy, cast out demons and perform miracles, all in the King's name? Take another look at what He said. "Many will say to Me on that day, 'Lord, Lord, did we not prophesy in Your name, and in Your name cast out demons, and in Your name perform many miracles?' And then I will declare to them, 'I never knew you; depart from Me, you who practice lawlessness.'"[6]

Years ago, while I was seeking to know more about the gifts of the Holy Spirit, I was desperately desiring to have an understanding of this passage of Scripture, and I sought the Lord for His answer. After all, what if I had full power and authority to do all these things, even the power to raise someone from the dead, what good would it do only to hear Him tell me to depart from Him because He never knew me? I simply had to know. And very gently and graciously He asked me if, as I stood before Him on the Day of Judgment, my words to Him would be, "Lord, did *I* not prophesy in Your name; did *I* not cast out demons; and did *I* not perform many miracles in Your name?" My response to Him was an immediate and emphatic, "No! He inquired of me what my response would be, and I remember telling Him that if I could at that moment get my face up off the ground as I bowed before Him, I

51

would say, "Lord, *You* allowed me to speak *Your* word; *You* cast out many demons; and *You* performed so many miracles! *You* were wonderful!" And He assured me that I had nothing to fear concerning this passage.[6]

Of the many parables Jesus the King taught concerning the Kingdom of God, the one that best teaches us to be prepared for His coming again to claim His bride is the parable of the ten virgins. While awaiting the coming of the King all ten took lamps to light the way to the wedding feast, but five of them were foolish and took no extra oil with them for their lamps, unlike the wise and prudent virgins who also took along their flasks filled with oil. The King delayed His coming, and in the process the lamps of the foolish virgins began to go out. The wise virgins were prepared to meet the King and went in with Him to the wedding feast.[7] (The feast in this parable was a prophesy of the wedding feast which was to come, referred to in great glory by the King to the apostle John while he was on the Isle of Patmos.)[8] The foolish five attempted to enter the celebration later but were refused. The lesson? Be prepared. Be filled with the Holy Spirit (the oil that keeps His fire burning within), listening for the voice of the King, ready always to greet Him and do His will.

An interesting example of this kind of preparation is found in the life of one Ananias, who was living in Damascus. In a vision, the King merely called him by name, "Ananias!" His immediate response was, "Here I am, Lord." Standing at the ready to do the bidding of his King, even though questioning Him about the wisdom of anointing Saul, he nonetheless carried out the King's instructions to the letter.[9]

Just how important is it to enter into the Kingdom of God? It is the singular most important step a person can take in this life. Many who heard the King wanted to follow Him, but there were those who first wanted to wait until they could care for, and perhaps bury their parents, and others who just wanted to be able to say goodbye to their loved ones at home. But when it comes to entering the Kingdom of God, the King will not take second place to anyone or anything.[10]

Several years ago, I recall a preacher of the Gospel telling of an incident where he had presented to a young man about to graduate from the Naval Academy the opportunity to meet the King and enter into His Kingdom. The cadet was very much interested, but decided to put it off until after his graduation. Before the day of graduation came, however, there was an unexpected and tragic accident, and the young man was instantly killed. The words of the preacher still ring in my ears at times. He said, "When you take one step away from the Lord, you are on your own!" The King indeed will not take second place.

To be sure, the King advises anyone desiring to enter His Kingdom to count the cost, for entering in is costly indeed. From the moment you enter in, the King becomes number one, over and above parents, children, siblings, spouse, and your very own life as you think you would like to live it. And the cross you will be called to carry, just as the King was required to carry His own, will not be an easy task. So be aware and prepared for the costs of following the King.[11]

In spite of the cost involved, there is no greater pursuit in life than that of pursuing the King and His Kingdom. Consider John, the baptizer. What a man of God! Jesus said of him while John was in prison awaiting his ultimate death at the hands of Herod Antipas that there was no one to that date who was greater than this prophet and messenger of God. And yet, the King also said that the one who is least in the Kingdom of heaven is greater than John.[12] Up until the time of John, the law and the prophets were preached and taught. Then John began proclaiming the Gospel of the Kingdom of God, and people began receiving the word and paying the cost by doing whatever was necessary to enter into the Kingdom.[13]

It is not easy to enter into the Kingdom of God. In fact, it is not easy to even see the Kingdom of God. There was a ruler and teacher of the Jews who recognized that Jesus had come from Father God, and he desired to know more about His Kingdom. The King told Nicodemus that unless he was born from above, or again, he would not be able to see the Kingdom of God. Not understanding, Nicodemus pressed in further, and the King told him that in order to enter into the Kingdom of God one would have to be born of water and the Holy Spirit.[14] This is the very message Peter proclaimed on the day of Pentecost when he said to those wanting to know what to do, "Repent, and each of you be baptized (immersed in water) in the name of Jesus Christ for the forgiveness of your sins, and you will receive the gift of the Holy Spirit."[15] In other words, you will be born from above and enter into the Kingdom of God. So, what will motivate one to believe, repent, and be baptized as the King commands? By the proclamation of the Gospel of the Kingdom of God.[16]

For the wealthy, the King made it clear that it would be especially difficult (but not impossible) to enter into His Kingdom. Why? Because of their concerns over possibly losing their wealth and property. In other words, placing more importance on their possessions and power than on the King and His Kingdom. One must be willing to give it all up for the sake of inheriting the Kingdom of God and living forever with the King. This lesson by the King must have been very important, for it was recorded for us in detail in three of the four Gospel accounts and referred to as the King's dealings with the rich young ruler.[17]

Of what exactly does the Kingdom of God consist—both in the present and in the future? Paul, an apostle, gives us what is perhaps the very best definition. In describing to us the way to live in the Kingdom by not judging one another as to what we eat or drink, he wrote, "for the Kingdom of God is not eating and drinking, but righteousness and peace and joy in the Holy Spirit."[18] Sounds pretty good, doesn't it? Peace and joy is that for which the world longs today, does it not? With the possible exception of certain radicals who would rather kill everyone who does not agree with them, most people of the world would prefer a path of peace and joy. Wouldn't it make sense to follow someone who loves us instead of hating us? And Paul would tell you that the One who loved you so much as to die for you is the one to follow, King Jesus.

However, His Kingdom is not just made up of peace and joy. There is the matter of righteousness. It is the same apostle who describes for us those who will *not* be in His Kingdom, now or in the future, unless of course they repent. It is a formidable list, so bear with me. To the churches of the province of Galatia, he wrote, "Now the deeds of the flesh are evident, which are: immorality, impurity, sensuality, idolatry, sorcery, enmities, strife, jealousy, outbursts of anger, disputes, dissentions, factions (or heresies), envying, drunkenness, carousing, and things like these, of which I forewarn you, just as I have forewarned you, that those who practice such things will not inherit the Kingdom of God."[19]

Adding to this list, Paul includes elsewhere such things as greed, filthiness, silly talk, and coarse jesting.[20] He goes on to say in another letter that instead of taking one another to courts of law, members of the Kingdom of God should rather be willing to be defrauded and wronged. Adding to this, he makes it clear that the unrighteous will not inherit the Kingdom of God, and describing those who are unrighteous he includes in this list fornicators, idolaters, adulterers, effeminate, homosexuals, thieves, covetous, drunkards, revilers and swindlers. None of these will inherit the Kingdom of God.[21] And, if these were not enough, to these lists the King, by way of His instructions to the apostle John, adds lying.[22]

The King Himself describes vividly just how important is this matter of righteousness in connection with His Kingdom. In essence, He states that any unrighteousness your hands or feet find to do, or your eyes tend to pour over, it would be better for you to cut out of your life anything which would cause you to be cast into hell, for there will be no unrighteousness or unrighteous acts in the Kingdom of God. This is a dire warning. Read it for yourself and decide on life in His Kingdom rather than the unbearable alternative.[23]

How different is life in the Kingdom of God as portrayed by Paul. For example, he writes that citizens of the Kingdom are to walk like Father God in love, goodness, righteousness, and truth. When one walks in the light, power, and authority of the Holy Spirit,[24] one will exhibit love, joy, peace, patience, kindness, goodness, faithfulness, gentleness, and self control.[25] Paul is quick to remind those in the Kingdom not to become so high-minded as to forget that they were rescued from some of the very acts and lifestyles of unrighteousness previously listed, those things which cannot exist in the Kingdom of God. After listing some of these things which are abominations in the sight of Father God, Paul writes, "Such *were* some of you; but you were washed, but you were sanctified, but you were justified in the name of the Lord (and King) Jesus Christ and in the Spirit of our God."[26]

By the Holy Spirit one is empowered to live the new kind of life in the Kingdom of God present that would otherwise not have been possible. Take a look at the Constitution of the Kingdom. Do you suppose that on your own you would be able to be the salt and light of the world? Or, without His help could you overcome your anger and hatred of others? Or, when slapped in the face could turn the other cheek? Or, learn to love and pray for your enemies and those who persecute you? Or, be merciful or humble? These are the things to which the King calls us, and by His example and the power of His Holy Spirit we are able to do. For these attributes and other characteristics like them amount to true Kingdom living.[27]

While it is helpful and exciting to explore the Kingdom of God past and the Kingdom of God future, we are in the present, and we need to see clearly the Kingdom of God present. But we might well point out that Jesus Himself, as He stood before Pilate, declared, as the King of the Jews, that His Kingdom was not of this world. In fact, He said His Kingdom was not from here.[28] And that, of course, was absolutely correct. His Kingdom never really was, is now, or ever will be, of or from this world as we know it. It is not a kingdom of the flesh, but rather is the spiritual Kingdom of God. In the King's prayer to Father God, He interceded for the citizens of His Kingdom (including you and me), asking His Father to protect them from all manner of evil and the evil one while they were *in* the world and stressing the fact that they were (and are not) *of* the world. Citizens of the Kingdom of God are to be one in the King and in Father God. The King is one with His Father and dwells in His people, and the people are perfected into one unified body.[29]

Of this mystery, and what a great mystery it was, Paul wrote, "the mystery which has been hidden from the ages and generations, but has now been manifested to His saints, to whom God willed to make known what is the riches of the glory of this mystery among the Gentiles, which is *Christ in you, the hope of glory.*"[30] This, saints, is the mystery revealed, the King in you and you in the King. This is the Kingdom of God present on the earth today.

How then is it possible to identify the Kingdom of God present? The religious leaders of His days on the earth wanted to know when this Kingdom was coming, and the King was quick to reply, "The Kingdom of God is not coming with observation, nor will they say, 'Look here or there.' For behold, the Kingdom of God is in your midst (or within you)."[31] What was He saying? First of all He was conveying to them the fact that the Kingdom of God was standing there in their very midst. He was the King, and His Kingdom resided in Him. Also, He was indicating to them that His disciples, in receiving Him as their King, were also receiving His Kingdom themselves. Did He not say to His disciples prior to this exchange with the Pharisees, "Do not be afraid, little flock, for your Father has chosen gladly to give you the Kingdom."[32]

It is one thing to receive the Kingdom of God, and quite another to know what to do with it once you have received it. To illustrate the point, the King shared another parable concerning what it means to receive His Kingdom. He related a story about a nobleman (in truth, Himself, the King) coming to a distant country to receive his kingdom. He then calls ten of his servants together, giving them each about one hundred days' wages, with instructions to use or invest these kingdom assets wisely until he returned. Upon his return he wanted an accounting for what they had done for his kingdom with these assets. One servant had increased his assets ten-fold, and another, five-fold. As a result the nobleman gave each of them increased authority in his kingdom. However, there was a third servant who was afraid to take any risks, and did not use the assets for the good of the kingdom at all. What authority had been given him was taken away, as was his place in the kingdom.[33]

The Kingdom of God and all its assets are to be shared, and those who have been given the Kingdom have responsibilities to the King. One of the perfect examples of this truth is found in the King's dealings with one of His closest companions, Peter. Upon the arrest of King Jesus this disciple denied even knowing his King, not just once or twice, but three times.[34] After His resurrection the King asked Peter if he loved Him, not just once or twice, but three times. The first two times He used the Greek word *agapao* for love. In other words, "Peter, do you love Me with an all-giving, no withholding, absolute love?" Peter was not yet able to reach that high bar in his relationship with the King, and so he answered by saying he loved the King, but using the Greek word for love, *phileo*, or brotherly love. The third time the King asked Peter whether he loved Him, the King lowered the bar for him and used the term *phileo*. And Peter was grieved in his heart that he could not then and there measure up to the King's expectations. Still, the King gave Peter the duty, responsibility, and authority to care for the lambs (newborn babes), and to shepherd and care for the sheep of the King's pasture (the older citizens).[35]

Oh, the time would come when Peter's love for the King would rise to the highest bar, for as history reveals to us, Peter, when facing death for his service to the King and His Kingdom, at and by his own request, was crucified upside down, not feeling worthy to die in the same manner as his King. He was not concerned for himself, but even in death wanted to honor his King.

What then is required of a true citizen of the Kingdom of God present? Much depends upon the calling the King has on your life. He indicated, for instance, that there would be those who would be called to be eunuchs for the cause of His Kingdom, and these would voluntarily serve Him in that capacity. The King was making it clear at one point that divorce between husband and wife, except for the limited cause of fornication, was not to be exercised in His Kingdom. His disciples at

the time were surprised at His teaching, and stated that if the relationship between a man and his wife were to be taken so seriously in the
Kingdom, that it might be better for them not to marry in the first
place. Whereupon the King stated that there would be those, no doubt
like the apostle Paul, who would be called upon by the King, to remain
single and not marry, all for the sake of His Kingdom.[(36)]

Paul referred to such a calling, and because of the then present or
impending distress of his day, recommended that unmarried men and
women remain in that condition. He also believed that by remaining
unmarried one could devote his or her entire time to the King and the
things pertaining to the Kingdom of God. He was quick to point out,
however, that what he was writing was according to his own opinion
by concession, and not by any command received from the King. He
was as quick also to point out that if a man or woman were already
married when apprehended by the King, they were by all means to
remain married. In addition, he clearly stated that it was not wrong
for the unmarried to enter into marriage with one another.[(37)] As an
aside, and not by any authority received from the King, if I am reading
the signs of the times in which we now live correctly, we may soon be
coming into a time of distress such as that described by Paul. If that be
true, perhaps it would be wise for the unmarried youth of our number
who may be contemplating marriage, to seek the face of the King to see
if He might have a special calling on their lives in the days ahead. More
perhaps about the signs of the times later in this treatise.

How then is one to receive the Kingdom of God, and who in that
Kingdom will be considered the greatest? Concerning the greatest in the
Kingdom, be certain that the ones seeking prominence or position in
the Kingdom of God for the sake of power and prestige will be greatly
disappointed. On one occasion the mother of James and John, the sons
of Zebedee, came to the King and unabashedly requested of Him to
command that her two sons be given positions of honor in His Kingdom,
one sitting on His right and the other sitting on His left. The other ten

apostles became indignant at her request. Why so? Perhaps because they too were looking forward to receiving such an honor. Just a thought!

In response to the request, the King wanted to know if James and John were able to drink from the same cup of sacrifice He was about to undergo. Without understanding the full impact of what He was asking them, I am certain, they were quick to reply that they indeed were able. The King assured them that they would indeed be called upon to suffer for the sake of the Kingdom, but that they did not understand the nature of authority and position in the Kingdom of God. Unlike how the rulers of the nations lorded it over their citizens, the King said, "It is not this way among you, but whoever wishes to become great among you shall be your servant, and whoever wishes to be first among you shall be your slave; just as the Son of Man did not come to be served, but to serve, and to give His life as a ransom for many."(38)

Apparently they, His disciples, like we today, were not quick to learn from the King's teachings. Not long before this particular incident, the King's disciples had approached Him with almost the very same question. They wanted to know who would be the greatest in the Kingdom of Heaven. At that time Jesus picked out a little child and placed him in their midst. He then said, "Truly I say to you, unless you are turned and become like children, you will not enter the Kingdom of Heaven. Whoever then humbles himself as this child, he is the greatest in the Kingdom of Heaven. And whoever receives one such child in My name receives Me."(39)

How is one to receive the Kingdom of God? With the innocence of a small child, humbly trusting in and following the King. Who will be the greatest in His Kingdom? The one who is the servant or slave of all, the one who is willing to lay down his or her own interests for the sake of the interests of others. How different from the worldly view, especially in this day in which we live.

In reading this perhaps you might be tempted to say that you have wasted far too much of your life; that you are too old to turn again and be like a small child in faith; that there really is no room for you in the

Kingdom of God. If you share any of these or similar thoughts, there is good news indeed for you. Turning once again to the parables of the King, there is one in particular which addresses those who might consider themselves to be a "Johnny-come-lately."

The King related a story of a man, a landowner, (again referring to Himself) who went out early in the morning to hire workers for his vineyard (Kingdom). He found some willing laborers, agreed with them concerning their wages, and put them right to work. Three hours later he found others available for work, but just standing idle. He hired them also and put them to work in his vineyard. At noon and again at 3:00 P.M. he found yet more available workers not yet working. Again, he hired them even though it was late in the day, and put them also to work in his vineyard. Finally, at about 5:00 P.M., he found still others who had been idle all day because no one had hired them. And he hired and put them to work also.

When the work day had ended, the landowner paid all of the laborers the same identical wage, beginning with those he had hired at 5:00 P.M. Some who had worked all or most of the day did not seem to think it was fair for those who had only worked for one hour to receive the same wage they were being paid, even though these same laborers had agreed that the wage offered them by the landlord was an acceptable wage. The landlord made it clear that if he chose to be generous to the late comers, it was his business and none of theirs'. The King concluded His parable with these words, "So the last shall be first, and the first last."(40)

In addition to a lesson on not to be envious or greedy, there is another valuable lesson in this parable. In the King's view, it is not too late for you to enter His Kingdom and receive the same wages, forgiveness of sins and life eternal with Him. And if that is what the King has said, who are you and I to argue with Him? So come, enter in!

Is there anywhere in Scripture of an example of anyone entering the Kingdom of God very late in life? So glad you asked! Do you recall when the King was hanging on His cross, shedding His blood in order to take away the sin of the world so that man could be set free from the law of sin and death? On each side of Him were two robbers who were condemned to death for their crimes. Both at first, along with many others in the crowd, were ridiculing the King. Then one of the thieves recognized that he deserved to die because of his crimes, but that the King had done no wrong, and did not deserve death. This one addressed the King with a personal plea in these simple words, "Jesus, remember me when You come into Your Kingdom." And the King replied, "Truly I say to you, today you shall be with Me in Paradise."[41] Imagine, being put to death for crimes committed, but at the same time entering life in the Kingdom of God by the authority of the King Himself!

In light of the above, one might be tempted to conclude that it is *never* too late to answer the invitation to enter into the Kingdom of God. That would be an unwise conclusion to draw, for it is also written, "Behold, now is the acceptable time, behold now is the day of salvation."[42] And, "Today, if you hear His (the King's) voice, do not harden your hearts."[43] There will finally come a day when the invitation is no longer offered because it has been rejected once too often. That is why the warning from Heaven is given. Listen carefully:

"See to it that you do not refuse Him who is speaking. For if those did not escape when they refused him who warned on earth, much rather we who turn away from Him who warns from Heaven."[44] The writer goes on to say there will come a shaking of the earth and the heavens. Everything capable of being shaken will be shaken. However, the Kingdom of God cannot be shaken. So, if you are not already in His Kingdom, do not delay to enter in and offer the King your acceptable service with reverence and awe "for our God is a consuming fire."[45]

Sadly, there will be those who reject the invitation to enter into the Kingdom of Heaven. By rejecting the invitation they will be rejecting the King and the One who sent Him, Father God. And, as the King advised the seventy disciples whom He sent out to offer the invitation, there would be cities where they would not be well received. With miracles being performed all around them they still would reject the King and

His Kingdom. What a horrible future they would face being brought down to the very depths of hell.[46]

What a privilege it is to proclaim the Gospel of the Kingdom of God. There is no greater honor or task given to those who are citizens of the Kingdom. Once apprehended by the King, Paul spent his entire existence boldly proclaiming the good news, reasoning and persuading people about the King and His Kingdom. This was true for him in Ephesus where he taught daily for a period of two years.[47] And as he was waiting death in prison in Rome, we still see him boldly proclaiming the Gospel of the Kingdom of God and presenting to all who would listen about the King, the Lord Jesus, the Christ, Messiah, Savior.[48]

What was it that propelled this servant of the King to spend his life trying to convince people everywhere, Jew and Gentile alike, to know the King and enter into His Kingdom? Hear the explanation from Paul himself:

> For if I preach the Gospel, I have nothing to boast of, for I am under compulsion; for woe is me if I do not preach the Gospel…For though I am free from all men, I have made myself a slave to all, so that I may win more. To the Jews I became as a Jew, so that I might win Jews; to those who are under Law, as under Law…so that I might win those under Law; to those who are without law, as without law…so that I might win those who are without law. To the weak I became weak, that I might win the weak; I have become all things to all men, so that I may by all means save some. I do all things for the sake of the Gospel, so that I may become a fellow partaker of it.[49]

Since there were times of impending distress during Paul's ministry propelling him on to complete the task given him by the King, perhaps it would be wise and fruitful for us in the Kingdom of God present to consider and compare the signs that the King set forth which would usher in the Kingdom of God future, especially as it relates to His coming again. Such will be the subject of Part Six of this treatise. Prior to beginning that segment may I strongly encourage you to read, study and meditate upon the words of the King in the three Gospel accounts of His teaching in which He describes events leading to the end of this age and the beginning of the next.[50]

In the meanwhile, may the church, the body of Christ the King, rise up to the challenge given it by the King Himself. And what is that? With the same passion and intensity of Paul, proclaim the gospel of the Kingdom of God to one and to all everywhere, in all times and seasons, so that all will hear and be given the opportunity of spending all eternity with the King in His Kingdom.

End of Part Five. Respectfully submitted for your study, prayer and consideration. November 23, 2006.

The Gospel
Part Six

N ow, as suggested earlier, let us take a look at the signs of the times, as revealed by the King, and compare at least some of those signs with what has happened since He spoke those words—and some which seem to be taking place before our very eyes today. The King began His teachings concerning these signs at a time when His disciples were enamored with the majesty and beauty of the buildings of the Temple. And in truth, what a sight it must have been to behold![1] What a shock it must have been to His listeners when the King announced, "Do you see these great buildings? Not one stone will be left upon another which will not be torn down."[2] The massive destruction of their beloved Temple occurred less than forty years after Jesus made this astounding declaration. His prophecy was true—all the more reason for us to carefully consider His other prophecies concerning the end of the age and His literal return to earth to begin the Kingdom of God future.

Before His coming again, He said there would be wars and rumors of wars, one kingdom of man rising against another.[3] History has certainly recorded for us a multitude of wars and threats of wars in the past two thousand years, including some in the lifetime of many of us still living today, such as two major world wars, the Korean conflict, and the war in Viet Nam, as well as hundreds of conflicts between kingdoms and nations. This nation has known a great civil war in its past, and there have been others in various parts of the world. All of these wars have taken their toll in the deaths and injuries of untold millions. And now the whole world seems to be involved in one of the most heinous of all wars, the war of terrorism.

Before we take a closer look at the current world conflict with terrorism, perhaps we need to consider some of the other signs which the King described—one of which interestingly enough He described as terrors. In this context He said that there would be earthquakes, plagues, famines, *terrors*, and great signs from heaven.[4] Who can deny the occurrence of many of these tragedies in the past few hundred years, such as the bubonic plague, devastating famines, and earthquakes. Someone no doubt will quickly point out that such tragedies have been with us down through the centuries. That certainly is true, but it is also true that more recently we seem to be flooded with great tragedies all over the earth. What plagues and diseases could be worse than the AIDS epidemic and Ebola, and now we are being informed that the avian flu could well wind up far surpassing in its intensity the massive deaths as those which resulted from the bubonic plague.

Who can question the horror of the pictures of those peoples suffering famine and starvation in Sudan and other African nations—as well as those in India and other Asian nations. To go on, what of the recent tsunami in the Far East—the explosion of recent eruptions of the so-called "Ring of Fire" volcanoes bordering on several continents and islands of the world. The regularity, intensity, and frequency of these, as well as, the devastating damage from hurricanes, tornadoes, floods, mud slides, and forest fires have increased in recent times one hundred times over. All of this plus the terror experienced and brought about by the violent acts of fanatic Islamists set off what has become the global war of terrorism.

Who could have imagined a war where the enemy would commandeer passenger jet planes full of innocent men, women, and children, crash them into the twin towers of the World Trade Center in New York City, into the Pentagon building in Washington, D.C., and attempt the same attack, this time aiming at either the national Capitol or White House—and later using similar tactics in Madrid, Spain, London, England, Bali, and elsewhere throughout the globe. The promised reward to these men for carrying out their missions? Forty virgins waiting for each of them in heaven! This is an enemy who uses their own wives, mothers, and children as shields, and even worse, straps explosives on them to commit suicide and mass murder, all in the name of Allah. Other than passenger planes and personal murder explosives, what is their main weapon? *Terror!* This is a war of evil against innocent lives, a war of enforced man-made religion versus freedom, the penalty for failing to convert to this false religion? Having one's head removed by use of the sword! How different is this from the invitation offered in love by the One who was willing to lay down His own life as a sacrifice for the sins of the whole world.

There will be at least one more major war after this present one before the coming of the King. Perhaps this present conflict will lead directly into the war which is yet to come. That war, referred to by many as the war of Gog and Magog, is described by the prophet Ezekiel where godless men form a great massive coalition of nations and come against the chosen people of Father God. Consider, if you will, the makeup of this evil force led by a nation coming from the far north and all these nations coming to destroy the nation of Israel. It will consist of Russia, together with what was once known as the nation of Persia, now known as Iran; Cush, encompassing what is today Ethiopia, Eritrea and Sudan; Put, including what today are the nations of Libya, Algeria and Tunisia; Gomer, which would probably include modern-day Turkey as well as some Germanic nations; Beth-Togarmah, which would no doubt include much of the old Assyrian empire, including at least what is now Syria, Lebanon, Jordan and northern Turkey, as well as Armenia, Georgia, Azerbaijan, and several of the so-called "Stan" nations of the former USSR. Quite a massive force of power![5]

What has not been discussed much, especially in the media until just recently, is that liaisons between these nations are already being formulated. Russia has personally entered into pacts, treaties, and contracts with many of the above kingdoms, as well as, other Arab nations such as Saudi Arabia, Yemen, Oman, Kuwait, and the United Arab Emirates. Once enemies, these nations now willingly share knowledge, expertise, and weapons of mass destruction—as well as the wherewithal to produce them in great quantities. The knowledge of what is really going on in the world today perhaps will prove to be a wakeup call to members of the Kingdom of God present as to just how near is this next major event to occur on the earth.[6]

If these things(with the possible exception of the coming war of Gog and Magog, which in my humble opinion will be far more severe than just the *beginnings* of birth pangs) were to be but the beginnings of birth pangs[7], for which other signs are we to look? The King said for instance that many would arise claiming to be Messiahs. Just recently the leader of Iran, President Ahmadinejad, boasted that the long-awaited Twelfth Islamic Imam was soon to make his appearance on the scene, and that he would lead the battle to destroy both Israel and America. Leaders of many beliefs, cults, and religious bodies have arisen proclaiming divine power and authority and speaking as though they themselves were gods.

The King warns His people not to be drawn in by these false messiahs and prophets performing great signs and wonders and directing you to go to secret places—either in inner rooms or somewhere out in the desert. They will be telling you that they have found the King. Just follow them. Don't believe it! When the King comes, the whole world will know it. What a magnificent spectacle it will be! And when you see Him coming in the clouds, look up and rejoice for your salvation draws near![8]

As to those false messiahs and prophets, one day they will come to know that the god from whom they derive their powers and authority is indeed a false god whose place in the abyss has been reserved for him—at first for a temporary sojourn of one thousand years during the reign on the earth of the King of kings and Lord of lords.[9] Once released from his pit, this false god will try yet once again, drawing multitudes to his side; but once again he will fail, and then he and those who followed him, including the anti-christ and the false prophet, will spend all eternity in agony in the lake of fire reserved for them.[10] That, of course, is at the time when the final and ultimate Kingdom of God future will make its appearance on the new earth!

Forgive me. Here I go again, getting way ahead of myself in the timeline of things to come! There have been multitudes of discussions, sermons, articles, and books on the theology of the end times. It indeed is an extremely important topic of study and understanding. Many have held that the return of the King is imminent, meaning He could return at any moment. Far be it from me to say when He can come and begin His thousand year reign on the earth. However, the King Himself has given us signs to look for in this regard, and, in my judgment, we ignore them at our own risk of misunderstanding the times. Shall we review some of the more obvious signs?

We have already very briefly discussed what appears to be one of the next major events on Father God's agenda for the world—the war of Gog and Magog against Israel. Without referring to this specific war in His end time discourse, the King did make specific reference to something His people in Jerusalem would personally be able to behold at a time prior to His return. He advised that they would see "the Abomination of Desolation which was spoken of through Daniel the prophet, standing in the holy place."[11] Since the King made specific reference to the words of the prophet, perhaps we should take a close look at what Daniel saw and wrote.

According to the prophecy of Daniel the Temple would be "built again—with plaza and moat—*even in times of distress.*"[12] This must be the Temple spoken of by Ezekiel, which *follows* the war of Gog and Magog, as referred to earlier in this treatise.[13] Daniel also wrote that after the building of this Temple, a prince would arise on the scene bringing with him a covenant of peace. Daily sacrifices will once again be restored to the altar of this new Temple, and they will continue for a period of three and one-half years. Following this period of time the prince will show his true colors, and instead of being the true Messiah King, he will prove to be the anti-christ. It is he who will stand in the holy place, the Temple, and by force do away with the daily sacrifices, desecrate the Temple itself, thus setting up the abomination that makes desolate.[14]

The King gave detailed instructions to those of His people then living in Judea when they see this abomination take place. Flee to the mountains! Don't look back! Don't be concerned about your possessions. Run for the hills, literally! If they were taking His advance warnings seriously, they were to begin to pray even then, and certainly now, that this time of desolation would not take place in the winter, making their escape more dangerous, or on the Sabbath, which would restrict how far they could travel on that day. And again comes the warning not to be taken in by false messiahs, prophets, and promises, because the coming of the King would come after this tribulation and would come with such signs from heaven that everyone on the earth would know of His coming![15]

From all these signs given by the King are we beginning to see a bit more clearly the time frame set forth by Father God and shared with us by the One He has anointed King—not only of Israel, but King of all the kingdoms of the earth? First there will be the devastating war of Gog and Magog together with its coalition. When Father God intervenes in that war, bringing total defeat to those coming against Israel, perhaps at that very time He will destroy the Dome of the Rock and the Al-Aqsa Mosque and clear the Temple Mount for the building of His Holy Temple. Ezekiel spoke these words of Father God, "It will come about on that day, when Gog comes against the land of Israel that My fury will mount up in anger. In My zeal and in My blazing wrath I declare on that day there will surely be a great earthquake (or shaking) in the land of Israel."[16]

At any rate, in summary, following the war of Gog and Magog, the next major event on Father God's calendar will be the building of His

Temple. Daily sacrifices in the morning and evening will be restored and practiced in this newly built Temple, and that will continue for some three and one-half years. The anti-christ will then reveal himself for who he really is, and will bring about three and one-half years of tribulation. And *then* the King will come in all His glory. Read the accounts again to see if the things spoken of by the prophets of old and the King Himself bear out these conclusions.

How it behooves the citizens of the Kingdom of God present to stay constantly on the alert. For the King warned not only that false prophets and messiahs would arise, but also that lawlessness would increase, and that the love of many would grow cold. And why will these things occur? Because great animosity toward the King, His Kingdom on earth, and His people in that Kingdom will rear its ugly head. He foretold how persecution of the saints of God would become rampant. Many, He said, would be taken before authorities and thrown into prison and delivered to tribulation for their beliefs and teachings, and many would even be killed for following their King. On a more positive note, He did tell them when the time came for those occasions, not to worry about what to say to the courts or authorities, for the words they were to speak would be given them at that very time by His Holy Spirit.[17]

Surely we are not so blind as to fail to see some of these very things happening all around us today. The persecution of Christians and Jews in Asian nations, such as China, Indonesia, India, Iran, and Russia are being constantly reported in religious journals and personal testimonies of the saints. And if in these nations there are such violent and flagrant actions being taken against the King's people, what of the Islamic nations where Christians and Jews are being beheaded for their faith.

Are we ignoring what has been taking place here in the United States in recent years? Prayer in public schools being eliminated, the reading of Scripture no longer permitted, prayers in the name of Jesus at graduation exercises and even football games being prohibited. All these decisions are not being made by the people or their representatives in Congress, but rather forced on the populace by a few judges of the various courts of the land. There have been demands for the removal of the Ten Commandments and of Christian or Jewish symbols and displays from public places—especially from court houses and municipal, state, and federal buildings. And again, these have not been decisions of or by the people of this nation, but rather imposed upon us by judges of federal and state courts. Add to this the assault against the laws of this nation which authorized the inclusion of the words "under God" in the pledge of allegiance to its flag.

The United States is in a cultural warfare between those who would be fully secular with no mention of the Creator God against what still amounts to the vast majority in the land who really want the freedom to express openly their faith in the Almighty and His plan for His people to live by—in short, the freedom *of* religion and not freedom *from* religion. The ACLU has become the chief spokesman for those demanding a purely secular nation. They seem to be prevailing far too often in the courts of our land against those desiring Judeo-Christian practices and values.

The public teaching of the Bible, both Old and New Testaments, has become for many strictly taboo. And yet at the same time demands are made for the teaching of Islam and the Koran in these same schools where instruction in the Bible is being denied. It is true that, at least for the moment in the United States, Christians and Jews are not being slaughtered wholesale for their beliefs, but so-called "legal" tape is being applied to their lips and tongues, effectively keeping them from freely proclaiming the Gospel of the Kingdom of God to the nation and to the world.

Is lawlessness increasing? It has been said that since 1973 in this nation alone some forty-three million babies have been murdered in and out of their mothers' wombs. Rapes, murders, perverted sex crimes, especially against children, have increased a hundredfold. Pornography, drugs, homosexuality, same sex unions... the list goes on. The things done and said under the guise of freedom of speech and freedom of the press is altogether abominable. Such is the price we pay for a secular society! And, woe to the one who cries out against these travesties. Yet there is hope for those who will cry out, sigh, and groan over all the abominations which are being committed in their midst. Those who will take a stand and speak out against these gross sins of mankind have the promise of Father God that they will receive His mark, the mark of life. Please read this account for yourself.[18]

Love of the many growing cold? Signs of this also are all around us. In the newly formed nation of Iraq we see Sunnis against Shiites, one Iraqi against another, each seeking power and/or revenge for past transgressions, and in the process literally thousands dying. Muslims in Turkey against the Kurds in Iraq. Arabs against Jews, and Jews fighting Arabs, and both coming into existence from the loins of a common ancestor, Abraham. In the world of so-called Christianity, Catholics and Protestants killing one another in Ireland; Roman Catholics against Eastern Orthodox Christians; and then there is the matter of some three thousand existing Christian denominations throughout the world—all fighting one another, and each claiming to be the one true church of the King! It is for this reason I do not hesitate to use the term "so-called Christianity," for do we not need again to be reminded that He said He would build His church(notice that He only promised to build one!) and that the gates of hell would not be able to prevail against it.[19] And, the truly sad part of the results of the tragedy of forgetting the second of the greatest of the commandments of the King, to love our neighbor as ourselves, there will be many in the Kingdom of God present who will fall away, betray others in the Kingdom, and wind up hating one another.[20]

In spite of all the above, there will be those who endure whatever the enemy has to throw at them. The remnant will persevere. And the King promises them that they will be saved.[21] The faithful will see to it that what the King has commanded will be done. The Gospel of the Kingdom of God will be proclaimed in the whole world as a testimony to all nations and peoples. Once accomplished, the King says then that the end will come.[22]

73

Surely someone will say that even the King said that no one knows the day and hour when He will come again, not even He Himself, but only Father God.[23] Quite true. However, He also told another parable in this regard. The King pointed out that when the fig tree puts forth its leaves and its branches are tender, you can tell that summer is near. "So you too, when you see all these things (the signs of the times He was referring to) recognize, or know that He (the King) is near, at the doors. Truly I say to you, this generation will not pass away until all these things take place. Heaven and earth will pass away, but My words will not pass away."[24]

The King sends this warning to all, to you and to me,

Be on guard, so that your hearts will not be weighed down with dissipation and drunkenness and the worries of life, and that day will not come on you suddenly like a trap; for it will come upon all those who dwell on the face of all the earth. But keep on the alert at all times, praying that you may have strength to escape all these things that are about to take place, and to stand before the Son of Man.[25]

We will close this Part Six with a promise of encouragement from the King. Even if the times of tribulation are indeed severe, and He has called you to endure them, take heart, because for the sake of His elect, His body, His church of both Jew and Gentile, the Kingdom of Heaven reinstated and restored to the earth, He will shorten those days of tribulation.[26] And the earth will truly, fully, and finally be invaded by God's heavenly realm. Praise the name of the King!

End of Part Six. Respectfully submitted for your study, prayer and consideration. December 10, 2006.

The Gospel
Part Seven

The Gospel, the good news of the Kingdom of Heaven having invaded the earth, and ultimately being restored to the earth in all its fullness, begins, as we have seen, with the birth of a baby in an animal shelter next to a filled-to-capacity inn somewhere in the town of Bethlehem. No ordinary baby was this. For this was the only begotten Son of God, born of a virgin, and destined to be the way for all who would believe in Him to become children of God.[1] This would be made possible by way of a rebirth provided, not by man, but by the will of God.[2] And those who would believe in their King would not only be allowed into the Kingdom of God, but would also, because of their intimate relationship with the King and Father God, become the recipients of the restored Kingdom of God in the earth.[3]

This baby was born King of the Jews;[4] and He would die King of the Jews;[5] and He would be raised from the dead as the King of kings and the Lord of lords. His Kingdom would be universal, because the King commanded, and continues to command, that this Gospel of the Kingdom of God be proclaimed to all the nations.[6]

When this baby was only eight days old He was circumcised as the law required, and later, as the first born son of Mary, was thus called to

75

be holy and dedicated to the Lord, as also required by the law, He was taken to Jerusalem and presented to Father God in the Temple. It was there that He was recognized by Simeon, under the influence of the Holy Spirit, as Father God's salvation for mankind, a light of revelation to the nations, and God's glory upon the chosen people of Israel.[7]

The next we know about the young King is when He is twelve years of age, about to become a man under Jewish tradition. We find Him once again in Jerusalem in the Temple discussing with the teachers of the day the things concerning Father God and astounding those teachers—as well as confounding Mary and Joseph with His understanding of, and the need for Him to be about, the things of His Father in Heaven. Jesus returned to Nazareth where He remained under subjection to His mother and stepfather until the time came for Him to begin His proclamation of the Gospel of the Kingdom of God.[8]

Why those years of silence from the One born to be King? The writer of the letter to the Hebrews supplies the answer. "Although He was a Son (the Son of God), He learned obedience from the things which He suffered. And having been made perfect, He became to all those who obey Him the source of eternal salvation, being designated by God as a high priest according to the order of Melchizadek."[9]

And so, we come to the time when John the baptizer identifies the King to all in his hearing as the Lamb of God who takes away the sin of the world and as the Son of God.[10] Jesus thereupon instructed John to immerse Him in water, even over John's protest that he, John, needed to be baptized by Jesus. When Jesus came up out of the water, the heavens were opened and the Holy Spirit descended from Father God and came upon the King, accompanied by the voice of His Father stating, "This is My beloved Son, in whom I am well-pleased."[11] Heaven invaded the earth once again, revealing the King of the Kingdom of God on the earth.

Following His temptation by Satan in the wilderness,[12] the ministry of the King officially began. He chose twelve disciples and began His journeys throughout all of Israel, bringing the good news(the Gospel) that the Kingdom of God had come from Heaven and had invaded the earth. He proved it time and time again by the miracles He performed and by the things He taught. And the subject of His teaching was always the same, the Gospel of the coming of the Kingdom of God to earth, its constitution, how to restore right relationship with Abba Father, how to receive forgiveness of sin, and how to gain eternal life. That was His Gospel, and that is the Gospel the members of His body are commanded to proclaim to a lost and dying world.

Consider again the parables taught by the King. Almost without exception they all described what the Kingdom of God was all about, and how to live in it. How His church needs to get back to the basics of returning to the King's messages, teachings, and prophesies instead of the teachings we have substituted for the true Gospel! Remember what the King said? "This *Gospel of the Kingdom* shall be preached in the whole world as a testimony to all the nations, and *then* the end will come."[13] Part of the model prayer the King taught us to pray was, "Your Kingdom come. Your will be done on earth as it is in Heaven."[14] Since He wants the Gospel of the Kingdom of God proclaimed to all nations in order for Him to be able to come again, should we not be about Abba Father's business—just like the King was always being about doing His Father's will?

The King spent three and one-half years proclaiming the Gospel of the Kingdom of God, and after accomplishing His assignment of the proclamation of this truth, accompanied by His healing the sick, lame, and blind, raising the dead, and delivering the oppressed from the demons of hell, He had but one more major work to do for Father God. He had to endure rejection by His own people, undergo an illegal trial, suffer indescribable pain and torture, and finally experience a death the likes of which cannot adequately be described or begun to be appreciated.

Knowing full well what would be required of Him, the King, while in the Garden of Gethsemane before His arrest, prayed a prayer of anguish to His heavenly Father. He was alone at this point, for His disciples, though requested by Him to keep watch with Him, had all been overcome with sleep and failed to provide Him with any comfort. Jesus prayed, "My Father, if it is possible, let this cup pass from Me, yet not as I will, but as You will."[15] Again, He prayed, "My Father, if this cannot pass away unless I drink it, Your will be done."[16] And, yet once again, He prayed the same prayer for the third time to His heavenly Father.[17] "And being in agony He was praying fervently; and His sweat became like drops of blood falling down upon the ground."[18]

What was this cup which the King did not want to drink? Was it the dread of having to undergo the agony of the crucifixion? As dreadful as that ordeal would be, that, in and of itself, was not the cup He was dreading. Jesus knew all along that He had to die in order to redeem the souls of mankind. And He even knew the manner by which He would have to endure that ignoble death. Consider these words of the King directed to His disciples, "Behold, we are going up to Jerusalem; and the Son of Man will be delivered(or betrayed) to the chief priests and scribes, and they will deliver Him to the Gentiles to mock and scourge and crucify, and on the third day He will be raised up."[19]

From where then does the deep anguish come which causes the King to sweat great drops of blood? His prayer in Gethsemane was not that He be spared from death, or even that He would not have to suffer that death in such a horrible way on a cross of wood, but rather His prayer was, "Let this cup pass from Me." Again we ask, what was the cup of which He so dreaded to drink? The cup was the cup of sin, and the cup of wrath which would come from a holy and just God. We cannot imagine the absolute agony, devastation, and horror experienced by the Holy One of Israel, whose lips had never once tasted of sin, to have to not just taste of the cup, but to drink down every drop of its contents, down to the last dregs; to take upon Himself and to be identified before Father God, as the very embodiment of all of the sins of every human being in the world, past, present and future. Finally, on the cross, the time comes when He has to drink this cup. And when He does, His Abba Father turns away from Him. Jesus has never before been separated from His Father. But as He drinks that cup the very presence of Abba Father is taken from Him! Anticipating this in the Garden of Gethsemane is almost too much for the King to bear. And when He actually does drink the cup on the cross, is it any wonder that He cries out in absolute agony, "Eli, Eli, lama sabachthani?" "My God, My God, why have You forsaken Me?"[20]

Yet, this is precisely what was necessary in order for the Kingdom of God and Heaven to be restored to the earth, and dominion of it to be returned to those who would repent and accept the forgiveness of sin and the Kingship of Jesus. "He (Father God) made Him (King Jesus) who knew no sin, to be sin on our behalf, that we might become the righteousness of God in Him."[21] God's love for man is beyond comprehension. We all have sinned against Heaven and Father God. The penalty for such sin under His law is death. And Father God in His absolute holiness, on the day of His wrath, has every right to cast us into hell. Instead we are told,

> But God demonstrates His own love toward us, in that while we were yet sinners, Christ died for us. Much more then, having now been justified by or in His(the King's) blood, we shall be saved from the wrath through Him(the King). For if while we were enemies, we were reconciled to(Father) God through the death of His Son, much more, having been reconciled, we shall be saved by or in His(the King's) life.[22]

Instead of giving us the justice we deserve, Father God grants to those in King Jesus His grace, mercy, and life eternal and restores the dominion over His Kingdom here on earth to His people. Why? Because King Jesus was willing to drink the cup of sin and take upon Himself the wrath of Father God—the wrath which we so richly deserve. That cup consumed by the King contained not only all sin in the world, but also the wrath of a holy and just God. That was the price which had to be paid to redeem mankind, deal the death blow to satan, and restore the Kingdom of God to the earth, granting dominion over it once again to mankind.

In the face of what the King would have to endure in order to set mankind free and restore to them the Kingdom of God on the earth, how could He possibly overcome the anguish which engulfed His very body, soul, and spirit in the Garden of Gethsemane? As difficult as it is to comprehend, He was able to overcome by the inner joy of knowing He was carrying out His Father's will and plan. *Joy?* Yes, *joy!* Look carefully at the words written by the writer of the Hebrew letter after describing the great faith of those existing down through the ages of time—those who were able to endure looking forward to the fulfillment of the promise that one day Father God would make all things right and restore His Kingdom here on the earth. They were not personally able to see that fulfillment in their day, but were convinced in their inward beings that it would come to pass. That is what faith is all about—"the assurance or substance of things hoped for or expected, the conviction or evidence of things not seen."[23] That is why the writer of this letter was able, by the authority and power of the Holy Spirit, to write,

> Therefore, since we have so great a cloud of witnesses surrounding us, let us also lay aside every encumbrance and the sin which so easily entangles us, and let us run with endurance the race that is set before us, fixing our eyes on, or looking to, Jesus, the author and perfecter of faith, who for the *joy* set before Him endured the cross, despising the shame, and has sat down at the right hand of the throne of God.[24]

The King could see the ultimate victory of Father God by His carrying out of Father God's perfect will, and in so doing the King has set the example for us to follow.

Part of the joy in the innermost being of the King was the knowledge of what had already been written about Him by another servant of Father God, Daniel, as he received by way of a vision from heaven:

I kept looking in the night visions, and behold, with the clouds of heaven one like a Son of Man(King Jesus) was coming. And He came up to the Ancient of Days(Father God) and was presented before Him. And to Him was given dominion, glory and a Kingdom(or sovereignty), that all the peoples, nations, and tongues might serve Him. His dominion is an everlasting dominion which will not pass away; and His Kingdom is one which will not be destroyed.[25]

And this Kingdom or sovereignty on earth would be restored to the people of God forever. The King and His saints (or holy ones) would have dominion over all the earth. This too was revealed to Daniel.

Then the sovereignty or Kingdom, the dominion and the greatness of all the kingdoms under the whole heaven will be given to the people of the saints or holy ones of the Highest One; His Kingdom will be an everlasting Kingdom, and all the dominions will serve and obey Him.[26]

As we bring to a close this treatise on the Gospel, the good news of the Kingdom of God restored to the earth and the people of God, let us see through the writing of another servant of Father God, Isaiah, as he was given the prophetic insight as to what would be required of the Son of God and the Son of Man, and what would be the result of His faithfulness in being obedient, even to death on the cross. As you will see, if indeed it is possible to comprehend, that it actually pleased Father God to crush His Son, causing Him to be made sin in our stead.[27] Follow with me as we consider how it would be possible for King Jesus to undergo such anguish, and yet with joy; and how it would please Father God to allow such suffering on the part of His Son. (Comments of this writer will be found in parentheses.)

Behold, My Servant will prosper, He will be high and lifted up and greatly exalted. Just as many were astounded at you(the people of God), so His appearance was marred, more than any man, and His form

81

more than the sons of men.(The appearance of King Jesus just before, during and following His crucifixion was indescribable, so horrible a spectacle was it.) Thus He will sprinkle many nations. Kings will shut their mouths on account of Him; for what had not been told them they will see, and what they had not heard they will understand.[28](His blood will redeem, and the truth will be made known.)

For He(King Jesus) grew up before Him(Father God) like a tender suckling, and like a root out of parched ground; He has no form or majesty that we should look upon Him, nor appearance that we should desire Him.(There was nothing about His appearance, as a baby, child or grown man that would demand people's attention.) He was despised and forsaken of men, a man of sorrows or pains and acquainted with grief or sickness; and like one from whom men hide their face He was despised, and we did not esteem Him.(His tortured body on the cross was unbearable to behold.) Surely our griefs or sickness He Himself bore, and our sorrows or pains He carried; yet we ourselves esteemed Him stricken, smitten of, or struck down by, God and afflicted.[29](What was actually reflected in His body on the cross was the horrible condition of sinful mankind.)

But He was pierced through or wounded for our transgressions, He was crushed for our iniquities; the chastening for our well-being or peace fell upon Him, and by His scourging(stripe) we are healed. All of us like sheep have gone astray, each of us has turned to his own way; but the Lord(Father God) has caused the iniquity of us all to encounter Him."[30](His entire appearance and condition reflected clearly our sins, rebellion and true spiritual condition.)

He was oppressed and He was afflicted, yet He did not open His mouth; like a lamb that is lead to slaughter, and like a sheep that is silent before its shearers, so He did not open His mouth.(Offering no defense or plea for Himself, the King gladly and with joy took our punishment on Himself so that we could be set free.) By oppression and judgment He was taken away; and as for His generation, who considered that He was cut off out of the land of living or life for the transgression of my people to whom the stroke(was due)?(No one realized that He was being crucified for the transgressions, sins, and rebellion of all the people of all the earth, past, present, and future, and not for any fault or guilt of His own.) His grave was assigned with wicked men, yet He was with a rich man in His death, because He had done no violence, nor was there any deceit in His mouth."[31] (He was considered to be as guilty as the thieves with whom He was crucified, and not worthy of a decent burial, but Father God arranged it so that His Son's body would temporarily reside in the grave of a wealthy man named Joseph from Arimathea, a disciple of the King, and a servant of Father God.)[32]

But the Lord(Father God) was pleased to crush Him(King Jesus), He made Him(the King) sick; if His soul would render Himself a guilt offering, He will see seed, He will prolong days, and the good pleasure of(or will of) the Lord(Father God) will prosper in His(the King's) hand. As a result of the anguish of His soul, He will see light and be satisfied; by His(Father God's) knowledge the Righteous One(King Jesus) My(Father God's) servant, will justify the many, as He(the King) will bear their iniquities.(It pleased Father God to crush His Son, King Jesus, because He had made the King to become *our* sin, though sinless Himself, and by His sacrifice the law of sin and death would be fully satisfied.) Therefore, I(Father God) will allot Him(King Jesus) a portion with the great, and He will divide the booty with the strong; because He poured out His soul to death, and was numbered with the transgressors; yet He Himself bore the sin of many, and interceded for the transgressors. [33]

Father God was pleased with His Son for His willingness to offer Himself up as our sin offering. God the Son drank the cup of our sin and died so that God the Father, as the holy and righteous God that He is, could be justified in receiving us again as His sons and daughters, and restore to us full dominion over His Kingdom here on earth.

Do you see it? It was Abba Father's good pleasure to crush His Son, who became the embodiment of our sin because He loved us so much! And it was the joy of King Jesus to become our sin offering because He loved the Father and us so much! The love of the Father was in Him, and the love of the Father is now poured out in the hearts of His people through the Gift that was and is given to believers, the Holy Spirit.[34] Father God poured out His wrath on His Son, King Jesus, so that by His blood we would be saved from the just wrath of a holy and righteous God, and be reconciled to Him, Father God, by the obedience of His Son.[35]

That, beloved, is the Gospel, the good news of the Kingdom of Heaven on the earth and its King. Hear it. Believe it. Respond to it. Be a part of it. And by all means, proclaim it!

End of Part Seven. Respectfully submitted for your study, prayer and consideration. January 4, 2007.

References

PART ONE

1. See Luke 1:26-33, esp. v.33
2. Luke 2:8-14
3. Genesis 3:14, 15
4. Daniel 9:25
5. John 1:29
6. See John 1:35-42
7. John 4:25
8. Psalm 24:7-10
9. Matthew 2:1, 2
10. 1 Timothy 6:15
11. Colossians 1:23
12. Mark 16:15-18; See also Matthew 28:16-20
13. Matthew 3:1, 2
14. John 1:29
15. Matthew 4:17
16. Matthew 13:16, 17
17. For the concept of Heaven actually invading earth, my thanks to Bill Johnson, author of *When Heaven Invades Earth*.

18. Matthew 4:23; 9:35; Luke 8:1
19. Matthew 5:3; Luke 6:20
20. Matthew 5:10
21. Matthew 13:11
22. Matthew 13:44
23. Matthew 13:45, 46
24. Luke 12:32
25. See Matthew 10:1-8; Luke 9:1, 2
26. See Luke 10:1-9
27. See Luke 10:17-24
28. Matthew 28:18-20; Mark 16:15-18
29. Acts 1:8
30. Matthew 24:14
31. Matthew 13:3-9; 18-23
32. Matthew 13:24-30; 36-43
33. Mark 1:14, 15
34. Mark 8:34 - 9:1
35. Acts 2:1-4
36. Mark 9:2-8
37. Matthew 13:34, 35
38. Matthew 13:44
39. Matthew 13:45, 46
40. See Matthew 6:25-34; Luke 12:13-34
41. Luke 12:32
42. Matthew 13:31, 32; See also Ezekiel 17:23; and esp. Ezekiel 31:6-9
43. See Matthew 13:33
44. See Matthew 13:47-50
45. Matthew 13:51
46. See Matthew 8:5-13
47. See John 20:24-29
48. Luke 2:8-14
49. Matthew 3:1, 2

50. Matthew 4:17

51. Mark 16:15

52. See Matthew 28:18-20

53. See Acts 1:1-3, esp. vs. 3

54. Acts 1:6

55. Matthew 16:18

56. Matthew 16:19

57. See Matthew 18:15-20

58. See Acts 1:4-8

59. Matthew 24:14

60. Acts 1:3

61. Acts 28:30, 31

PART TWO

1. Matthew 16:18, 19

2. See 1 Corinthians 1:1-3; 2 Corinthians 1:1, 2; Galatians 1:1-3; Ephesians 1:1; Philippians 1:1; Colossians 1:1, 2; 1 Thessalonians 1:1; 2 Thessalonians 1:1, 2; Titus 1:5

3. Matthew 28:18

4. John 17:20-23

5. See 1 Corinthians 12:12-27

6. See Matthew 21:23-46

7. Matthew 21:43

8. See Genesis 15:5; 22:17; 32:12; Hebrews 11:12

9. Genesis 18:21

10. See Genesis 32:24-32; 35:9, 10

11. Genesis 35:11, 12

12. Genesis 15:13, 14

13. See Exodus 19 and 20

14. Genesis 15:14

15. Exodus 19:5, 6

16. Exodus 19:8

17. See 1 Samuel 8:1-9
18. 2 Samuel 7:8-17
19. See 1 Kings 3:6-15
20. 2 Kings 18:1-7
21. 2 Kings 22:1, 2
22. See 1 Samuel 15:1-29
23. See 1 Kings 12:25-33
24. See 1 Kings 16:21-26
25. See 1 Kings 21:1-29
26. Deuteronomy 18:15; Acts 7:37
27. Matthew 21:10, 11; Luke 7:16,17
28. Psalm 110; Hebrews 2:17; 4:14-16; 5:4-10
29. Psalm 24:7-10; Isaiah 43:15; Jeremiah 10:6, 7; Matthew 2:1, 2; 27:11; John 12:15; 1 Timothy 6:13-16
30. Matthew 23:13
31. Matthew 21:43
32. 1 Peter 2:9, 10
33. Galatians 3:28, 29; 1 Corinthians 12:13; Colossians 3:11; Romans 10:12, 13
34. Study Ephesians 2:1-22

PART THREE

1. 2 Corinthians 5:17-20
2. Matthew 3:2; 4:17
3. Matthew 10:1-8; Luke 9:1, 2
4. Luke 10:1-9
5. Matthew 28:18-20; Mark 16:15-18
6. See, e.g., Luke 10:9; Matthew 10:1, 8; Luke 9:1; Mark 16:17, 18; Matthew 11:1-6, esp. vs. 5
7. Matthew 28:18-20
8. John 3:16
9. Compare Matthew 22:1-9 with Luke 14:16-24

10. Acts 2:36, 37
11. Acts 2:38-40
12. Acts 2:41
13. See Acts 8:14-17
14. See Acts 10:1-48
15. Matthew 16:13-19
16. See Colossians 1:13, 14
17. See Isaiah 43:10-13; 45:5-7; Psalm 90:2
18. Job 38:4; See also Isaiah 42:5; 45:18; Revelation 4:11
19. Genesis 1:1
20. See Luke 2:9-14; Jude 9; Isaiah 6:2, 6; Genesis 3:24
21. Isaiah 6:1-5
22. See Genesis 1:27-30
23. See Genesis 1:29; 2:9, 19-22
24. Genesis 2:16, 17
25. See Genesis 2:16, 17; 3:1-24
26. Genesis 2:16, 17
27. Genesis 3:22-24
28. Genesis 5:5, 20, 27
29. 2 Peter 3:8
30. See "A Visit With Grandpa" a short treatise by the author, unpublished, but provided on request
31. Genesis 5:24
32. Genesis 6:5-7
33. See Genesis, chapters 6 through 10; esp. 6:8, 17-22; 7:1-5; 9:11-17; See also 1 Peter 3:18-22
34. See Genesis 11:1-9, with emphasis on "Us" in vs. 7
35. See Acts 2:1-12
36. See Genesis 12:1-7; 13:14-18
37. See Genesis 17:1-9
38. Genesis 17:7
39. See Genesis 21:1-8
40. Genesis 12:1-3

41. See Genesis 16
42. See Genesis 21:9-20
43. Genesis 24:60
44. Genesis 25:23
45. Genesis 35:11, 12
46. See Genesis 37:1-27; also chapters 39 through 45
47. Genesis 12:5-7
48. Genesis 46:2-4; See also Genesis, chapters 47 through 50
49. Genesis 15:13, 14
50. Exodus 3:10; See also Hebrews 11:23-29
51. See Exodus 3:11-14:31; esp., 14:31; See also Hebrews 11:23-29
52. Exodus 16:35
53. See Numbers, chapter 11
54. Exodus 19:4-6
55. Exodus 19:8
56. See Exodus 20:2-17; Deuteronomy 5:6-21
57. See Matthew 22:36-40; See also Deuteronomy 6:5; Leviticus 19:18; Galatians 5:14
58. Exodus 24:3, 7
59. See Exodus 32:1-14
60. See Exodus 33:9, 11, 14; Exodus 40:34-38
61. See Numbers, chapters 13 and 14; also Deuteronomy 1:25-39
62. See Deuteronomy 1:1-8
63. Deuteronomy 1:37, 38; And See Deuteronomy 3:23-28; Deuteronomy 31:23
64. See Deuteronomy 20:1-4; Joshua 1:1-9
65. See Joshua 1:3, 4
66. See Judges 2:10-16; 3:9-11
67. See Judges 3:12 - 16:31
68. Judges 21:25
69. 1 Samuel 3:20; 7:15; 8:1-9
70. See 1 Samuel 8:10-22
71. 1 Samuel 9:2, 16

72. 1 Samuel 10:1, 6, 9, 24

73. 1 Samuel 13:8-14

74. 1 Samuel, Chapter 15

75. 1 Samuel 16:1, 11-14; See also 2 Samuel 5:1-5

76. 2 Samuel 7:16

77. See 2 Samuel, chapter 11; and 2 Samuel 12:1-23; See also Psalm 51, for example, of true repentance

78. 1 Kings 1:32-34

79. See 1 Kings 3:5-14

80. See 1 Kings 6:1-38, esp. vs. 12, 13; See also 2 Samuel 7:5-16; 9:2-5

81. 1 Kings 9:6-9

82. See 1 Kings 11:1-13; Matthew 24:1, 2

83. See, e.g. I Kings, chapter 12; 1 Kings 14:22-24; 15:1-3; 15:25, 26; 32-34; 16:25, 26; 30-33

84. 1 Kings 15:8-15; 2 Kings 12:1, 2; 2 Chronicles 17:1-19; 2 Chronicles 20:1-30; 2 Kings 18:1-7; 2 Kings, chapter 22 and 23:1-25, esp. vs. 25

85. 2 Chronicles 36:18-23; Ezra 1:1-4; For an in-depth study of this adventure, read the Books of Ezra and Nehemiah.

86. For the best coverage of the King's dealings with His people and their enemies, as well as the ultimate promises for the future, see especially the books of Isaiah, Jeremiah, Ezekiel and Zechariah

87. Malachi, chapter 4.

PART FOUR

1. Psalm 145:13

2. See Daniel 2:37-44, esp. vs. 44

3. Psalm 22:28

4. Psalm 24:1

5. Psalm 24:7-10

6. Matthew 5:5

7. Matthew 25:31-34
8. Matthew 6:10; Luke 11:2b
9. See Revelation 19:11-16; Ezekiel 34:22-24
10. See Revelation 20:1-6
11. See 1 Thessalonians 4:16, 17
12. 1 Corinthians 15:50-57
13. See Acts 1:1-11, esp. vs. 11b
14. Zechariah 14:4, 5b, 9; inserts by me
15. Daniel 7:13, 14
16. Revelation 1:7; See also Zechariah 12:10-14
17. Isaiah 9:6b, 7
18. Daniel 7:27; See also Isaiah 32:1; Revelation 3:21; 5:10; 22:5-7
19. See Isaiah 2:2-4; 33:22
20. Isaiah 11:4, 5; 24:23b
21. Ezekiel 37:15-28; 39:25-29; See also Isaiah 11:10-13
22. See Isaiah 19:17-25, esp. vs. 23-25
23. See Isaiah 35:8-10; 62:10-12
24. See Isaiah 11:6-9; 65:25
25. See Isaiah, chapter 60, esp. vs. 1, 3, 5, 10a, 12, 14, 15, 21, 22
26. Zechariah 2:10, 11
27. See Isaiah 61:10, 11; Ephesians 2:4-22; Galatians 3:26-29
28. See Isaiah 65:17-25; See also Zechariah 8:1-8, esp. vs. 4, 5
29. See Ezekiel 47:8-12
30. Zechariah 6:12, 13
31. 1 Corinthians 3:16; 6:19, 20
32. 1 Peter 2:5
33. Zechariah 14:9, 10, 20, 21
34. See John 19:26, 27; Mark 9:2
35. Revelation, chapters 21 and 22
36. Psalm 110:1; Matthew 22:43, 44; Mark 12:36; Luke 20: 42, 43; Acts 2:34, 35; Hebrews 1:13; See also Hebrews 8:1, 2; 10:12, 13; 12:2
37. 1 Corinthians 15:20-28

38. Revelation 21:1-4
39. Revelation 21:27
40. Revelation 22:2
41. Revelation 22:3, 4
42. Revelation 22:7, 11-14

PART FIVE

1. See Matthew 5:17-20
2. Compare Mark 12:28-34, esp. vs. 34, with Matthew 22:36-40
3. See Matthew 7:13-23
4. See Luke 11:14-23
5. Matthew 10:1; Luke 9:1, 2; 10:1,9,17; Mark 16:15-18
6. Matthew 7:22, 23
7. See Matthew 25:1-13
8. See Revelation 19:1-8
9. See Acts 9:10-17
10. See Luke 9:57-62
11. See Luke 14:25-35
12. See Matthew 11:7-11; Luke 7:19-29
13. Luke 16:16; See also Matthew 11:12; and esp. Acts 14:21, 22
14. See John 3:1-8
15. Acts 2:38
16. Acts 8:12
17. See Matthew 19:16-30; Mark 10:17-31; Luke 18:18-30
18. Romans 14:17
19. Galatians 19:21
20. Ephesians 5:3-6
21. 1 Corinthians 6:1-10
22. Revelation 21:27
23. See Mark 9:43-48
24. See Ephesians 5:1, 2, 8, 9
25. Galatians 5:22, 23

26. 1 Corinthians 6:11, (emphasis and parentheses mine)
27. See Matthew, chapters 5, 6 and 7
28. See John 18:33-37
29. See John 17:1-26, with special emphasis on vs. 6, 11, 14, 15, 16, 18, 20-26
30. Colossians 1:26-28
31. Luke 17:20, 21
32. Luke 12:32
33. See Luke 19:11-26; See also Matthew 25:14-30
34. See Matthew 26:69-75; also John 18:15-18, 25-27; Mark 14:66-72; and Luke 22:54-62
35. John 21:15-17
36. See Matthew 19:3-12, esp. vs. 11, 12
37. 1 Corinthians 7:6-11, 20, 24-28, 32-38
38. See Matthew 20:20-28
39. Matthew 18:1-4; See also Matthew 19:13-15; Mark 10:13-16; Luke 18:15-17
40. Matthew 20:1-16
41. See Luke 23:39-43; Matthew 27:44
42. 2 Corinthians 6:2b
43. Hebrews 4:7b
44. Hebrews 12:25
45. Hebrews 12:28, 29
46. See Luke 10:1-16
47. See Acts 19:1-10
48. See Acts 28:30, 31
49. 1 Corinthians 9:16-23
50. Read Matthew 24:1-51; Mark, chapter 13; and Luke 21:5-36

PART SIX

1. Mark 13:1; Luke 21:5
2. Mark 13:2

94

3. Matthew 24:6, 7

4. Luke 21:11

5. Read Ezekiel, chapters 38 and 39; See also Rosenberg, Joel C., *Epicenter*, chapters 8 and 9

6. Luke 21:11

7. Matthew 24:8

8. Matthew 24:23-31

9. See Revelation 20:1-3

10. See Revelation 20:7-10

11. Matthew 24:15; Mark 13:14

12. Daniel 9:25

13. Ezekiel, chapters 40 through 47

14. See Daniel 9:26, 27; 11:31-33

15. See Matthew 24:15-31; Mark 13:14-27; Luke 21:20-28

16. Ezekiel 38:18, 19; See also *Epicenter*, by Joel C. Rosenberg, chapter 13, esp. p. 188

17. Luke 21:12-15; Mark 13:11

18. See Ezekiel 9:1-11, esp., vs. 4

19. See Matthew 16:13-19

20. Matthew 24:10

21. Matthew 24:13

22. Matthew 24:14

23. Matthew 24:36 ,42, 44

24. Matthew 24:32-35

25. Luke 21:34-36

26. Mark 13:20

PART SEVEN

1. See John 1:12

2. John 1:13; See also John 3:1-8

3. Luke 12:32

4. See Matthew 2:1, 2

5. See John 19:14-22; also Matthew 27:37; Mark 15:26; Luke 23:38
6. See Luke 24:45-47; Matthew 28:18-20; Mark 16:15, 16
7. See Luke 2:21-32
8. See Luke 2:41-52
9. Hebrews 5:8-10; See also Philippians 2:5-11
10. John 1:29, 34, 36
11. See Matthew 3:13-17
12. See Matthew 4:1-11
13. Matthew 24:14
14. Matthew 6:10
15. Matthew 26:39; See also Mark 14:36; Luke 22:41, 42
16. Matthew 26:42
17. Matthew 26:44
18. Luke 22:44
19. Matthew 20:18, 19
20. Matthew 27:46
21. 2 Corinthians 5:21
22. 1 Corinthians 10:16, 17
23. Hebrews 11:1
24. Hebrews 12:1, 2
25. Daniel 7:13, 14
26. Daniel 7:27
27. See Isaiah 53:10-12
28. Isaiah 52:13-15
29. Isaiah 53:2-4
30. Isaiah 53:5, 6
31. Isaiah 53:7-9
32. See John 19:38-42
33. Isaiah 53:10-12
34. Romans 5:5; See also, as a blessing, Luke 11:9-13
35. See Romans 5:8-11

Recommended Reading and Listening

Biblical quotes and references taken from the New American Standard Bible: The Lockman Foundation, LaHabra, CA, 1977

Bright, John. *The Kingdom of God.* Nashville/New York: Abington Press, 1953

Howes, Mary Ruth, ed. 365 *Days with E. Stanley Jones.* Nashville, TN: Dimensions for Living, 2000

Johnson, Bill. *When Heaven Invades Earth.* Shippensburg, PA: Destiny Image Publishers, Inc., 2005

Jones, E. Stanley. *The Unshakable Kingdom and the Unchanging Person.* Nashville/New York: Abington Press, 1972

Mains, David. *Thy Kingdom Come.* Grand Rapids, MI: Zondervan Publishing House, 1989

McBirnie, W.S. *Keys to the Kingdom.* Lake Mary, FL: Creation House, 1991

Mumford, Bob. *The King and You.* Old Tappan, NJ: Fleming A. Revell Co., 1974

Munroe, Myles. *Rediscovering the Kingdom.* Shippensburg, PA: Destiny Image Publishers, Inc., 2004

Pryor, Dwight A. Audio teachings: Jesus, John the Baptizer, and the Kingdom of God; and Kingdom Confusion, Kingdom Challenge: Center for Judaic-Christian Studies, www. jcstudies.com

Rosenberg, Joel C. *Epicenter*. Carol Stream, IL: Tyndale House Publishers, 2006

> *The Copper Scroll*. Carol Stream, IL: Tyndale House Publishers, 2006

> *The Ezekiel Option*. Carol Stream, IL: Tyndale House Publishers, 2005

Snyder, Howard. *The Community of the King*. Downers Grove, IL: InterVarsity Press, 1977

> *A Kingdom Manifesto*. Downers Grove, IL: InterVarsity Press, 1985

Soleyn, Sam. *The Kingdom of God, A Series*. Adapted from messages given on Prime Time Christian Broad-casting Network, http://www. soleyn.org: 1995

Please visit my website at www.kingdomoftheking.com

Pleasant Word

To order additional copies of this title call:
1-877-421-READ (7323)
or please visit our Web site at
www.pleasantwordbooks.com

If you enjoyed this quality custom-published book,
drop by our Web site for more books and information.

www.winepressgroup.com

"Your partner in custom publishing."

Printed in the United States
117871LV00012B/291/P